Faith and Freedom

Faith and Freedom

THE MORAL CASE FOR AMERICA

Sven R. Larson

RESOURCE *Publications* • Eugene, Oregon

FAITH AND FREEDOM
The Moral Case for America

Copyright © 2019 Sven R. Larson. All rights reserved. Except for brief quotations in critical publications or reviews, no part of this book may be reproduced in any manner without prior written permission from the publisher. Write: Permissions, Wipf and Stock Publishers, 199 W. 8th Ave., Suite 3, Eugene, OR 97401.

Resource Publications
An Imprint of Wipf and Stock Publishers
199 W. 8th Ave., Suite 3
Eugene, OR 97401

www.wipfandstock.com

PAPERBACK ISBN: 978-1-5326-7931-5
HARDCOVER ISBN: 978-1-5326-7932-2
EBOOK ISBN: 978-1-5326-7933-9

Manufactured in the U.S.A.   JUNE 13, 2019

To my first grandchild;

May you live in liberty

Contents

Preface: Why I Wrote This Book ix
a. The ideological battleground xi

1 Libertarianism: America's Past, America's Future 1
a. Human imperfection and American liberty 5

2 Social Justice and the Commodification of Liberty 8
a. Egalitarianism and social justice 10
b. From social justice to commodified liberty 14
c. From commodified liberty to the welfare state 16

3 From the Welfare State to Tyranny 19
a. Forced labor 20
b. Utilitarianism 23
c. Rule by moral decree 28

4 Foundations of American Liberty 31
a. The individual and the minimal state 33
b. Libertarianism vs. Objectivism 36
c. Charity as a moral obligation 41

5 Corruption of the Social Fabric 44
a. Politicizing private life 45
b. The inevitability of conflict 47
c. A life ensconced in the welfare state 49
d. Uncertainty 52
e. The moral fallacy of the closed system 55

6 Challenging American Liberty: Property Rights 58
a. Parliamentary democracy vs. the constitutional republic 60

    b. The dangers with parliamentary democracy 62
    c. American liberty jeopardized: Kelo v. New London 68
    d. Subordinating property rights to social justice 70
    e. Public purpose: egalitarianism in the Fifth Amendment 74
    f. Appendix 77

7 Challenging American Liberty: The Welfare State 81
    a. Economic development: a tool for social justice 82
    b. Beyond the Fifth Amendment 85
    c. The Marxist roots of public purpose 88
    d. Social justice at work 93

8 Social Justice vs. American Liberty 97
    a. Three phases of ideological transformation 97
    b. Texas v Azar 102
    c. Inherent conflict: the iron law of wages 104
    d. Foundations of the welfare state: the relative definition of poverty 109
    e. Marxism and social justice in the federal budget 115

9 Restoring American Liberty 120
    a. Utilitarianism and the public purpose 121
    b. Christian public policy in practice 127
    c. When the welfare state fails 129
    d. Work ethic: providing for our families 134
    e. Paid leave: an overview 136
    f. Work ethic and financial security 138
    g. The FFA and government tax revenue 143
    h. Stewardship and charity: a reform idea 145
    i. Welfare reform done right 148
    j. Value through selflessness 153

In Conclusion 157

References 159

Preface
Why I Wrote this Book

> Once unquestioning obedience, once fully enslaved
> Once fully enslaved, no nation, state, city of this earth,
> ever afterward resumes its liberty.
>
> *Walt Whitman*

WE CAN TAKE CARE of ourselves, our loved ones and our communities, and we can do it without government. No matter how benevolent, government always imposes a heavy hand of rules, regulations and costs, direct and indirect, on whomever it takes care of.

Wherever freedom is tried, it prevails. Wherever freedom prevails, everyone prospers. For example, it is far better to be poor in the United States than in North Korea. Beyond the obvious material differences, every American has the chance to better his life on his own terms.

That is not to say America is without challenges. She is indeed: her legacy from almost 250 years is in jeopardy to a degree not experienced by any previous generation. Time is running out on the greatest nation in human history, and the fault is not an outside enemy. The fault is within: her own people has morally abandoned her.

If America loses her legacy, she loses her future. Once gone, she will not come back. The prosperity, the liberty, the human ingenuity—and the moral values that were embedded in America's founding—would all be lost. The repercussions on the world would be unimaginable.

Preface

I wrote this book to make my contribution to this country and its future. As an immigrant, I know better than most what difference America still makes in people's lives. Therefore, I also know the depth of the loss that we would all suffer if we abandon this country, culturally, economically—and morally.

For a quarter of a millennium, America has stood as a beacon of freedom to the rest of the world. She provides tremendous opportunities for us, as she has for hundreds of millions of people before us. But she is so much more than just individual freedom and opportunity. America is an endeavor, a constantly evolving project, preserved, defended and improved upon by every generation. She is handed down from parents to their children, not as an entitlement, but as a moral duty to balance the right to liberty with a responsibility to care for, improve upon and respect.

America is a source of inspiration, showing mankind what we can aspire to. America embodies the very essence of what it means to be created in the image of God. Thanks to the steadfast faith of the Founding Fathers, and their belief that the unleashing of God-given talents is the only path to freedom and prosperity, America offers the chance of a better future for people of all walks of life, and all walks of faith.

This is not just a rhetorical pastiche. It is what this country was founded to be, it is what she has been for the past 250 years. It is what has attracted people to come here, rather than to countries founded on competing values.

There is no question what America has been. The question is what she will be in the future. Will she remain the same nation, the same common cause for all of our posterity, a hundred years from now? I worry that she won't; that me and my generation of immigrants will be the last who could build a new, better life here as opposed to where we came from; that we will be the last ones to get to explore our potential in America as others before us have known her.

I have written this book in defense of the country I sought to become part of. My defense is not an exercise in the social sciences, let alone politics. I am not making a case for any particular political faction. Instead, I am making a case for the foundation of the American experiment in civilization; for the ideas that built her, that generations have inherited, preserved, improved upon and passed to others to care for.

My case for America is a moral case. It is meant to set focus on where we as a nation came from, to shed light on the ideal that inspires people

Preface

around the world, either to try to come here or to improve upon their own countries.

To make my case, I also contrast America's founding values against her greatest adversary:

- On the one hand, the values that founded America place the individual above the state;
- On the other hand, the values that challenge her place the state above the individual.

The moral case for America is a case for a project of human achievement, based on the belief that we are all endowed with liberty by our Creator. It is a project that does not limit liberty to any particular group, whether religious, racial or other, but extends it to all men and women. It is a project that has not been easy, but a struggle and a constant fight for growth and improvement.

Throughout her first quarter millennium, America has aspired to live up to the moral ideals planted into her founding documents; to make American liberty a reality for all. She has made great strides, stumbled, gotten up and pressed on.

There are those who are willing to give up on America, to have her morph into a nation like any other. I am not one of them. I believe that America is exceptional, and for a good reason. America is not perfect, but nothing man-made can ever be perfect. What matters is not how close we are to perfection, but how determined we are to continue to improve upon the American experience.

This book is my case for the continued progress and improvement of this great country. It is also my case against the ideas that have put our nation's character, future and prosperity in danger.

The Ideological Battleground

If the ideological foundation of America could be summarized in one term, it would be "American liberty". It captures the unique combination of inspired wisdom of our Founding Fathers. That wisdom combined Christian faith with Enlightenment values of individual sovereignty. Formulated as Christian public policy and libertarianism, these two channels of intellectual inspiration led to our nation's founding documents: the Declaration of Independence and the Constitution.

Preface

America's ideological adversary can also be conveniently summarized. Its term is "social justice". This is not to say that the ambitions of those who promote social justice are anti-America; on the contrary, many people who fight for social justice truly believe their cause to be in line with the values that are uniquely American. Rather, "social justice" is the ideological opposite of America because of its political practice. Policies in its image, while well intended, have repercussions that force us as a country to, eventually, choose between the liberty and opportunity that America offers, and the egalitarianism and entitlement of social justice.

Despite the ambition of social-justice proponents to fit both into one country, it is not possible. American liberty and social justice are mutually exclusive in their political practice. However, their incompatibility does not start there; it ends there. The clash between the ideologies behind the two concepts begins at the philosophical level. They represent opposite sets of moral values, opposite theories of the individual and the state, and diametrically different notions of liberty and justice.

Egalitarianism, the ideology behind the term "social justice", is utilitarian in both theory and practice. It views the individual as subordinate to the state; liberty and justice are quantifiable concepts where one person cannot gain more without someone else losing in equal amount. By contrast, American liberty originates in God-given natural rights, places the individual above the state and explains liberty and justice as fully extendable to all, without mutual individual exclusion.

A conversation between the two ideologies is crucial to America's future. Egalitarianism has made such deep inroads into our country's socioeconomic fabric that as we approach our nation's 250th birthday, we are forced to make a choice: do we proceed just a little further down the path of social justice, and fundamentally remake our country in the image of an egalitarian, European welfare state? Or do we acknowledge the errors of the egalitarian ideology; do we recognize that American liberty is better for all—not just those who are well off—and chart a new course to restore the values upon which this country was founded?

To answer this question, we need to understand, in depth, how the egalitarian ideology and American libertarianism are absolutely mutually exclusive. This is not a simple matter; in fact, when egalitarians and libertarians try to communicate, the conversation often cannot even land in a common analytical framework:

- To the egalitarian, what matters from a policy viewpoint is the end result of economic activity, colloquially who gets to spend the money. Therefore, the moral question that egalitarian policy is supposed to address is about economic redistribution.
- To the libertarian, what matters is the voluntary exchange between free individuals of economic resources; the outcome of gainful trade.

This makes the two ideologies prescribe entirely different policies. The egalitarian sees government intervention into private lives as not only a necessity, but a virtue of government; the libertarian, on his end, sees such intervention as an impediment, a vice.

If the argument stopped here, the default conclusion would be to find common ground between the two ideologies, one where government plays some role of modifying the outcome of free-market economic activity. However, the differences are of such depth that America as a country, a moral cause, a civilizational experiment, cannot proceed based on an attempt to let the two live side by side. The primary reason for this is that the egalitarian pursuit of social justice is not limited in its scope: its political nature is not one of a big government, but one of an expanding government. Social justice exists as a legislative phenomenon by the trend in government, not its size.

At the heart of the difference between American libertarianism and egalitarian social justice is the difference between utilitarianism and natural rights. These two moral value theories are mutually exclusive: a moral value cannot be founded in both utilitarianism and natural rights at the same time. The difference between them determines their differences all the way from abstract theory to policy recommendations and legislative practice; morality opens a door for public policy to enter the economy at different points, depending on what value theory one chooses to rely on.

The libertarian, whose value theory is natural rights, believes morality enters the economy in the exchange of resources between individuals. So long as exchange is voluntary; so long as the economy is based on the principles of the free market; exchange between individuals is voluntary. Whatever the outcome of that exchange may be, it is moral.

The egalitarian, by contrast, enters morality into the economy at the point where money is spent. The definition of morally acceptable spending is based on its distribution between individuals—people's spending is moral or immoral depending on the spending by each individual relative to

Preface

other individuals. He is led to this conclusion by means of his value theory, utilitarianism, which guides him to value the consumption by two people in relation to one another.

Since the policy practice of egalitarianism necessitates comparison of individuals, the egalitarian needs an instrument—a yardstick—by means of which he can make the comparison independently of how the individuals perceive their own situation. To do this, in turn, the egalitarian needs to equip the state to perform such comparisons, not only with the measurement tool but also with the authority to accordingly alter people's personal finances.

By equipping the state with utilitarian policy-making tools, the egalitarian elevates the state above the individual. The individual is subordinate to the state.

It is here, in the relation between the individual and the state, that American liberty and egalitarian social justice become mutually exclusive. It is also here, in this relation, that America's ideological battleground has opened up, with the egalitarian trying to establish the state as superior to the individual and the libertarian striving to restore the opposite relationship.

Acknowledgements

A BOOK IS NEVER produced in isolation. It is, rather, an amalgamation of experiences and interactions that an author has over an extended period of time. This book is no exception. However, unlike my previous books, this product came to fruition not so much through traditional research within my profession—political economy—as through thoughts, readings and writings in pursuit of a broader context.

Perhaps logically, the experiences and conversations that have led me to this book are less tangible than in normal, scholarly circumstances. I have felt a need to write this book for many years, longer than I realized when I eventually sat down to write it. Therefore, the strings of inspiration that led me here, stretch far back in time, in some cases to people who are no longer with us.

Perhaps the most pivotal source of inspiration was Sven Grassman, a Swedish economist who was my instructor when I wrote my undergraduate thesis in economics. I also had the privilege of working with him on various research projects for several years.

If I took anything away from those years, it was to never accept conventional wisdom and to always find ways to let policy be informed by principles—no matter how big the gap may be between reality and your ideals. In Grassman's case, those principles led him in a different ideological direction than I have chosen, but his unrelenting belief that principles can guide us right, no matter how big the obstacles, have inspired me throughout my professional career.

Sadly, he passed away many years ago.

I also want to thank my libertarian friends, first and foremost Dan Mitchell, Michael Tanner and Chris Edwards, for many inspiring conversations over the years. Like me, they toil in the trenches of public policy, trying

Acknowledgements

to make a difference over the long term in an increasingly short-sighted world. Their dedication, commitment and intelligence always inspire me to do better, to ask more questions and—when possible—find more answers.

There are numerous people whom I have never met, but whose work I am indebted to: philosophers like John Rawls and Robert Nozick; economists like John Maynard Keynes and F.A. von Hayek; and principled politicians as disparate as President Ronald Reagan and Congressman Dennis Kucinich. They were all men who stood up for principles and beliefs and sought to find ways to turn those principles into real-world change.

I owe a lot to Father Michael Smith of St Peter's Anglican Church in Cheyenne. Not only did he provide valuable comments on an early version of this manuscript, but he also continues to bring me and my wife in contact with our Lord. Father Michael's thoughtful sermons have been truly inspiring in my work on this book.

There are many others whose thoughts, questions and challenges have allowed me to make this book better than it otherwise would have been (and all remaining flaws are of course attributable to me alone). My good friend Susan and her unrelenting belief in founding principles as a guidance to innovative policy solutions; my children, with their unending quest to make the most of the American dream; and, of course, my dear wife Christina, whose love, intelligence, humor and patience with my workoholism continue to amaze me.

Last, but definitely not least: my unending thanks to our Lord Jesus Christ for inspiring me to become a better man.

1

Libertarianism

America's Past, America's Future

To say that the Constitution of the United States is a libertarian document is to set one self up for ire from both conservatives and egalitarians. The former will decry libertarianism; the latter will decry the constitution. On libertarianism, conservatives agree economically but disagree socially; egalitarians take the exact opposite position. On the constitution, conservatives see it as validating their values while egalitarians refute its lack of protection of economic entitlements.

In their criticism of libertarianism and the Constitution, both sides imply that libertarianism is not the ideological foundation of our constitution. Despite being surrounded by critics, libertarians can still lay claim to its only ideological foundation. However, their defense of it has been wavering of late: libertarians have allowed the public perception of their ideology to be distorted into a narrow advocacy forum for egalitarian social issues. While it is certainly true that a person's private life is his matter, and his matter alone, the advancement of gay marriage and other social issues have narrowed down the conventional wisdom of libertarianism.

Economic issues have fallen to the wayside, leaving libertarians ill equipped to counter the most consequential form of government growth: the welfare state. Whether this is for lack of interest among libertarians, or for a fundamental misunderstanding of libertarian ideology, is not important; of significant consequence, though, is the fact that ignoring or being ignorant of the conditions of economic self-determination leaves the libertarian practically unarmed in the battle over the role of government in the economy—and in people's lives.

This meaning of libertarianism is more relevant to the constitution than any other ideological principle. It is, in fact, the key to understanding why the constitution ranks the individual above the state. In doing so, the constitution places the responsibility of self-determination on the individual, while also granting him the liberty to pursue it to the best of his skills, his abilities and his preferences.

Here, libertarianism is inspired by Christian public policy. This inspiration is not coincidental, nor is it limited to political ideology. It is as much a matter of political practice. The Founders were informed by God's word, which they channeled into public policy with precision and dedication not seen either before or after. They distilled the principles of liberty from the Biblical prescriptions of individual freedom and responsibility, combining it with the libertarian theory of the minimal state. In doing so they formed the unique blend of public policy that is American liberty.

Alas, it comes as no surprise that libertarians have been the most successful of all ideologists in defending the U.S. Constitution, especially against egalitarianism on the ideological battle ground of our time. A good example of such a libertarian defense is a 1956 article by Charles Wolfe of the Foundation for Economic Education. Titled *Libertarians and the Constitution*, Wolfe's piece explains:[1]

> [Toward] the end of the nineteenth century, and especially since the 1930s, more and more Americans began to accept a theory of government—call it statism, collectivism, socialism, or what you will—in direct opposition to the individualist philosophy of our Founding Fathers.

Libertarians, Wolfe says, are the most able defenders of the values upon which our Constitution is built. They are, namely,

> rooted in a clear perception of the significance of the individual, his inclinations toward self-sufficiency and self-government, and his deep beliefs in the right to own and exchange the fruits of his labors without government intervention.

Wolfe sees a clear connection between libertarianism as a theory and the Constitution as political practice. This is now a radical, even controversial conclusion, especially given the advances of egalitarianism and

---

1. See: https://fee.org/articles/libertarians-and-the-constitution/

growth in government during the 20th century. In fact, already at the time of Wolfe's essay government had outgrown its ideological confinements as established in the constitution. Two significant examples are the federal income tax, enacted in 1913, which Wolfe mentions, and Social Security, President Franklin Roosevelt's signature peacetime achievement.

Properly understood, libertarianism provides the best possible lens through which to interpret the ideological challenge to American liberty that is the welfare state. Such interpretation is quintessential to the very survival of America beyond her approaching 250th birthday. The ideological battle is configured around the gap between libertarian theory and the practice of government. This gap, in turn, is created by an egalitarian ideological wedge, driven into our country by a relentless pursuit of social justice.

In fact, since Charles Wolfe penned his essay, the nature of government in American life has changed so profoundly that the nation itself is on the brink of once and for all severing its ties with its founding values and documents. Again, with Wolfe's words, the libertarian has the greatest responsibility of all ideologues in defending, restoring and preserving American liberty for future generations. That responsibility, again, includes a thorough understanding of the egalitarian adversary to our nation's founding values. That adversary was observable to Charles Wolfe and the libertarians of his time, but it had not yet reached the state of policy practice.

Today, egalitarianism has reshaped the very purpose of American government. Its path from ideological values to actual policy is no longer shrouded in a veil of political mystery. The flag of social justice was raised above our nation less than a decade after Wolfe wrote his essay; ever since the start of the War on Poverty in 1964 American liberty has been gradually watered down and marginalized. In its place, the principles of social justice and economic redistribution have gained steadily more ground, to a point where they are now poised to define our nation's ideological character.

American liberty will not longer be exceptional; it will be an exception.

The practical nature of this ideological transformation cannot be understated. With the War on Poverty and steady egalitarian advancement, the pure functions of government—protection of life, liberty and property—have been reduced to a budgetary residual. Today, two thirds of the federal government budget go toward spending programs that redistribute income among American families. In other words, two thirds of the budget put egalitarian theory into practice. Programs like Medicaid, temporary assistance, federal housing and food stamps are designed to redistribute income and consumption among America's families.

To consolidate the encoding of egalitarianism into American law, Congress changed the very definition of poverty.[2] Government was assigned an entirely new role, one that required it to permanently intrude on the finances of some citizens in order to permanently benefit others. Taxes are no longer used for the limited purposes of law enforcement and national defense, not even for last-resort poverty relief programs. They are now spent on a comprehensive reconfiguration of the American economy, in the image of egalitarianism and social justice.

Early elements of the welfare state appeared long before the War on Poverty. Already by the late 19th century the United States had *de facto* created a compassionately conservative version of the welfare state. With the War on Poverty, the welfare state was radically reconfigured in the image of the Scandinavian, and in particular the Swedish template. For the first time in our nation's history, egalitarian values were encoded into law. It was economically entrenched by means of permanent, steadily growing entitlement programs.

Unless defenders of American liberty learn to defeat egalitarianism in practical policy reforms; unless they summon the fortitude to take their ideology from theory to practice in a systemic fashion that sizes up the entire welfare state; American liberty will not longer be the prime character trait of this country. Libertarianism and egalitarianism cannot coexist under the same flag. Over time, one has to give way to the other. As an immigrant from Sweden, perhaps I see this better than many others. Having done what millions have done before me, come here to build a better life, I have something to compare to that most Americans don't: an egalitarian past. I can extrapolate that past: once egalitarianism is encoded and fiscally institutionalized, the nation's future is by default going to be egalitarian. Only a determined and systematic challenge by libertarians and their fellow defenders of American liberty, will change our nation's egalitarian destiny.

So far, the egalitarian conquest of America has been slow and gradual. At the same time, libertarians in general have exhibited an irresponsible lack of analytical prowess in their counter strategy. The combination of their weakness and the slow egalitarian progress has for the most part allowed the transformation of the United States to proceed without much meaningful resistance.

2. See Larson (2018).

Therefore, the very idea that the welfare state is antithetical to America and her constitution is still alien to the public discourse. There have been occasions of overt and systemic libertarian resistance: the fight over the Affordable Care Act—Obamacare—slowed the egalitarian progress toward one of its coveted goals, namely a single-payer health care system. However, such a temporary setback will not ease the conflict between two mutually exclusive ideologies. It will somewhat delay the inevitable choice that we have to make as a nation, but that is all.

Human imperfection and American liberty

The work to save American liberty begins with a reconnection with the values embedded in the American founding. Those values are not just important to our country but to the world. The project that the Founding Fathers created aimed to liberate people in ways they had never been liberated before, first and foremost in the Colonies, secondly later generations and peoples across the world, by means of inspiration and competition with traditional, authoritarian forms of government. For the first time, a nation was designed to constrain government, not individuals. As British philosopher and constitutional theorist D.J. Bentley noted, the uniqueness of the American founding lay in the idea that people consent to be governed.[3]

In addition to recognizing the formidability of our nation's founding, defenders of American liberty need to overcome a destructive habit that has even spread into the layers of libertarians: to take the fruits of liberty for granted. It is easy to become a consumer of the achievements of previous generations. The laurels earned by those who came before us make for a comfortable bed, from which it is easy to become a habitual critic of America's shortcomings. However, to point to flaws in our nation's past; to criticize the Founding Fathers for having only built an imperfect union, without making meaningful contributions to the restoration and preservation of American liberty; is to reduce oneself to triviality.

It is easy to enjoy the freedom and peace provided by more than 200 years of Americans, to consume historic levels of economic progress and take one's current existence for granted. It is a simple task to spy on history from hindsight, to point to the lack of universal suffrage and the existence of slavery in 1776 and dismiss the historic accomplishments of the Founders.

3. See Bentley (1973).

It is unremarkable to enjoy the fruits of prosperity while looking down on those who put their very lives on the line to lay the foundations of that very same prosperity. To criticize America's history for what it lacks is to arrogantly demand perfection of the Founding Fathers. As exemplary men as they were, they were not perfect—but unlike their modern-day critics, they knew they were not perfect. They had no illusions about the nation they created; they knew it was not without flaws.

Perhaps the most profound mistake that America's critics readily make, is to not realize that the Founders never aspired to solve every problem of their time. As much as they wanted to do more, they had to align their nation-creating ambition with the limitations that tyranny and uncertainty place upon the human existence. What they accomplished was outstanding in their time: they created not a perfect Union, but a *more* perfect Union.

The Founders knew that America would be an ongoing project, that she would take steps forward, that she would stumble, suffer setbacks and get up and move forward again. Their gift to the future was not a perfect nation, because—again—nothing man creates can ever be perfect. Instead, their gift to us was a set of historically unique tools; political, legal and cultural institutions that we could use on our journey through the American experience. The Founders gave us an opportunity to build on their legacy, to show that we could be responsible stewards of their creation; that we would not just consume what we inherited, but add something to it.

This point is more than just a reminder of the nature of human imperfection. It is a premise for the very choice between two futures: one built on American liberty, and another based on egalitarianism and a life ensconced in the welfare state. The latter is based, namely, on the fundamentally non-American idea of human perfection. Ideologies that promise a socio-economic vision where government corrects the outcomes of human action, are ideologies that believe in human perfection. That belief, in turn, gives birth to the ambition to end history. As opposed to great men and women in our past and our present, who strive for the gradual improvement of human life and human society, those who believe in human perfection promise to correct historic errors once and for all.

The stronger this belief, the more radical the ambition to end history.

The ambition to end history runs a bulldozer through individual freedom. It is human choice, and human imperfection, that create the prosperity and opportunity that free societies offer. It is also human imperfection that gives rise to the problems that those striving to end history want to solve. Yet, in order to end history, man must expand government to the point where no aspect of human life is left to chance or choice.

It is a sad yet inescapable fact that many, if not most, of our nation's problems originate in the arrogant and ignorant belief in the perfect man. When man thinks of himself as a conduit for perfection, he will find a way to create perfection. He will invent the tools that he thinks let him rise above his fellow men as the one to correct all the flaws, faults and failures of history.

Since imperfection is human, those who desire to create perfection need to re-engineer the lives of their fellow men. Only by altering the way we live our lives can they end imperfection—and history. The tool they use to remove imperfections from other people's lives is government.

Instead of trying to engineer away human nature, the men behind the American founding aspired to limit the impediments that our own imperfection place in our way. They gave us the instruments to secure that the libertarian values in the Constitution would free all of us from the shackles of government.

First and foremost, that included ending slavery, which was brought to an end within a century of the nation's founding. From there, America has continued on her path to gradual improvement.

Striving for improvement, for betterment, is the libertarian way forward; believing that we—unlike everyone before us—can create perfection is to choose the egalitarian route to history's end. To understand the difference is to preserve American liberty for the future. By contrast, to fail to understand this difference is to spell the end for our nation as we, our ancestors and our Founding Fathers have known her.

2

Social Justice and the Commodification of Liberty

FOR ALMOST A CENTURY, egalitarianism has defined the economic and cultural evolution of the Western world. In the first half of the 20th century, egalitarian thinkers produced plans for systemic reforms of entire nations. Some of them, like revolutionary communist leader V.I. Lenin, inspired violence and open tyranny. In good part thanks to Lenin, the Soviet empire oppressed hundreds of millions of people and deprived them of even the most basic of freedoms.

Outside the openly tyrannical iterations of egalitarianism, the most elaborate and politically most successful plan for societal transformation was written in Sweden. Its influence, however, has stretched beyond the Swedish borders, through more than 80 years. The plan, written by economist Gunnar Myrdal and his wife, sociologist Alva Myrdal, was published in 1934. It laid out an elaborate scheme for how to fundamentally transform Sweden from a traditional European country to a centrally planned economy with a fully developed egalitarian welfare state.[1]

Over a period of about 20 years, from the late 1930s to the end of the 1950s, the social democrat government implemented the Myrdals' plan, step by step. Sweden underwent the most radical social and economic transformation of a Western nation outside of the Soviet sphere. It extended government presence into almost every dimension of human life: health care,

---

1. The book, the Swedish title of which is *Kris i befolkningsfrågan*, has never been translated into English. It was first introduced to an English-speaking audience in Larson (2018).

child care, education (from kindergarten through college), general income security, retirement security, elderly care, housing and transportation.

Government sought to, once and for all, solve all problems in society. The pace and scope of the reforms was such that by the late 1960s, leading Swedish social democrats declared that all major problems in society had been solved.

History had come to an end.

At the time, this confident declaration of egalitarian victory seemed convincing. In 20 years' time, the Swedish social democratic party had peacefully transformed the country so thoroughly that it changed the very way Swedes lived their lives. Entire neighborhoods, even cities, were physically and economically designed around egalitarian principles. Government set a standard for acceptable housing, then practically monopolized the housing market. It created a single-payer health care system that dictated who could get what health care, and when—as well as who were to be denied what care, and why.

The societal master plan decided what child care children got, and what they learned while in government care. The plan actively sought to minimize the role of parents starting already at a child's birth. Government decided where children went to school and what they were taught. The master plan also gave government full control over people's retirement and provided general income security during the active years in the workforce.

All these needs were no longer the responsibility of the families and individuals themselves; they were now provided for by government.

For as long as American egalitarians have envied Sweden for what they see as a masterpiece society, others have feared it for much the same reasons. Their fear is warranted: the Swedish egalitarian welfare state, which was imported to America in the 1960s, is in every aspect antithetical to the American founding. It gives government almost complete responsibility for people's lives, reversing the relationship between the individual and government. Where the American constitutional republic puts the individual above government, the egalitarian welfare state puts government above the individual.

The contrast between the United States the Founders created and the Swedish egalitarian welfare state, is a contrast between two mutually exclusive political ideologies. It is the contrast between American liberty and social justice as policy strategies.

Many American egalitarians are confident that there can be an egalitarian America. Foremost among them is the late political economist John Kenneth Galbraith. Throughout a rich and impressive authorship, he often expressed his firm conviction that America could indeed survive—and thrive—by importing the Swedish welfare state.

Hard-line egalitarian politicians like Senator Bernie Sanders share Galbraith's belief. Sanders and his followers evidently think that a vast expansion of government and the welfare state would in fact be an improvement of America.

To prove the error in this belief, an examination is necessary of both ideologies: American liberty blending libertarianism with Christian public policy; and egalitarianism which manifests itself in the political pursuit of social justice.

Egalitarianism and social justice

Egalitarian ideology was given prominent form in the works of philosopher and Harvard professor John Rawls. In the mid-1970s his theory of justice became a staple of American progressive political thought, and it remains the unsurpassed definition of egalitarian political thinking.

Over a span of 14 years, from 1957 and his article *Justice as Fairness* to 1971 and the publication of his highly influential book *Theory of Justice*, Rawls developed a philosophical, ideological argument for egalitarianism in America. His theory of justice—really a theory of *social* justice—has become almost iconic among the American left and given them plenty of fuel in their pursuit of an egalitarian remake of America.

From the viewpoint of the left, Rawls filled a vacuum in political thought just a hair to the right of openly totalitarian socialism. His work did not explicitly seek to endorse any particular policies, but for all intents and purposes it provided a philosophical endorsement of the egalitarian ideology that built the Swedish welfare state. It was in the image of this ideology that America's progressives began transforming the country in 1964 with Lyndon Johnson's War on Poverty.

Rawls showed up at the right time for America's left. Galbraith, the economist, was politically more influential and analytically more astute, but his writings were dense and inaccessible to the more airy minds on the left. There were also passages in Galbraith's books that could be construed as taking economic reforms farther than what was palatable even for American liberals of the mid-20th century. He more than hinted of support for central economic planning, even though he himself would probably have denied it. Nevertheless, the mere thought of associating liberal reforms in America with a staple of Soviet socialism was enough to raise a barrier between Galbraith's contributions and many on the left.

This did not take anything away from Galbraith's influence. He made a difference in no small part as advisor to four presidents. Rawls, a philosopher, came across as intellectually more accessible to many, with writings that were well suited for refined dinner conversations.

More importantly, his theory of social justice gave the illusion that egalitarianism was compatible with the American constitutional republic.

In reality, egalitarianism and American liberty are mutually exclusive. The egalitarian transfers the decision on what is an appropriate use of economic resources from the individual who earns or provides those resources, to government. By necessity, this means that government is ranked superior to the individual: if, and only if, the individual is reduced to an instrument of government policy, can Rawls's egalitarian theory of social justice work in practice.

The American Constitution, by contrast, ranks the individual above government: the very founding of the United States is based on the principle that government, not individual liberty, should be restricted.

Egalitarianism is to the American founding what water is to fire, yet its proponents still try their best to make them work together. Their efforts concentrate on finding common ground with the Founding Fathers over two concepts that are essential to the ideology of the Constitution: justice and liberty.

From a practical policy viewpoint, justice is the most consequential of the two concepts. Rawls demonstrates this by centering his entire argument for an egalitarian society around a re-definition of justice. It is, he says,[2]

> a virtue of institutions constituting restrictions as to how they may define offices and powers, and assign rights and duties; and not as a virtue of particular actions, or persons.

This short paragraph is an attempt to suggest that people have the right to influence the conditions of their own everyday lives, but it is formulated in such a way as to elevate the triviality of this point to a thoughtful intellectual exercise. However, its almost platitudinal message fills an important

---

2. See Rawls (1957).

purpose in Rawls's theory: to put his skeptics at ease before he presents his real, ideologically significant definition of justice. This definition spreads the concept of justice so thin across human life that it eventually loses its meaning:

> justice is the elimination of arbitrary distinctions and the establishment, within the structure of a practice, of a proper balance between competing claims.

To make this definition work in practice, Rawls has to extend the concept of justice to include an entirely new subdivision. We know that subdivision as "social justice" and it is quintessential to the political practice of egalitarianism. When Rawls says "elimination of arbitrary distinctions" he means that nobody should be able to benefit from any advantage they were born with or inherited. For example, a tall person should not make more money playing basketball than the average person would on the same basketball court. By the same token, a person who was brought up with good work ethic should not be paid more than the person working next to him who is late and lazy.

By broadening the concept of justice to include social justice, egalitarians can claim that their definition of justice is not at all antithetical to the American founding. After all, it is still justice. However, the incompatibility between American liberty and social justice is revealed as soon as social justice is put to work in public policy. The only way it can work, namely, is by violating the fundamental constitutional principle of individual liberty.

The problem originates in Rawls's definition of "social justice" as saying that nobody should benefit comparatively from their background. This also means that nobody should suffer comparatively from their background. Two children, growing up next door, should not be different from one another in any aspect they cannot control; if Jack's parents force him to do homework before he can play, while Joe's parents do not care, then Jack should not get better grades or have a more successful career than Joe.

At a systemic level, this means no more, no less than a society where there literally are no economic differences between individuals. To work in practice, Rawls's social-justice theory thus necessitates a society and an economy that does not allow an individual to either benefit or suffer from his individual characteristics. Neither work ethic and risk-taking nor sloth and indolence can be permitted to make a difference to a man's fortune in life.

Social Justice and the Commodification of Liberty

A society that meets Rawls's criteria for social justice is an egalitarian society.[3] Political philosopher and Reed College professor Peter Steinberger elegantly explains what this means.[4] He uses an example where there is high demand for construction workers willing to build skyscrapers. Most people suffer from fear of heights, excluding them from those jobs, thus creating a situation where there is excess demand for high-rise construction workers.

Rawls's theory of social justice prohibits economic differences between risk-taking construction workers and those who choose the safest possible jobs, as well as between hard-working construction workers who are highly productive, and those who show up late for work, perform poorly and add much less value per hour worked.

Steinberger's example demonstrates that there are only two venues for economic redistribution in compliance with Rawls's theory:

1. The egalitarian welfare state, where progressive taxes finance a welfare state that redistributes income and consumption from high-income earners to low-income earners; or

2. Central economic planning, where wages and prices are dictated by government and the distribution of goods and services has nothing to do with people's preferences or wants.

Intuitively, it is easy to agree that children should not suffer from what parents they have, but it does not follow that economic redistribution is a workable or preferable remedy. On the contrary, the pursuit of social justice inevitably comes into open conflict with individual freedom. A welfare state cannot provide the resources it promises, unless those resources are produced in the first place. The welfare state itself disincentivizes that production. When men are rewarded without regard to their work, the welfare state incentivizes people to be idle; the less they work, the more they are entitled to. Since the principle of social justice prescribes benefits to people without regard to their reason why they are not providing for themselves, it does not matter if a man chooses not to work or is unable to.

Simultaneously, the theory of social justice implies—but, in Rawls's terms, does not explicitly endorse—marginal income taxes that place the brunt of the tax burden on the shoulders of high-income earners. The continuation of disincentives from entitlements and this tax-based

---

3. See Arrow (1973).
4. See Steinberger (1989).

disincentive formulates a society where idleness gradually outweighs workforce participation.

Rawls does not prescribe a solution to this problem, probably because he does not foresee it. Yet there is only one solution, namely a workforce participation mandate. To maintain the welfare state, government will eventually have to force people to work, or else the welfare state will not be able to deliver on its entitlement promises.

When the welfare state cannot deliver, social justice has no meaning; when the welfare state forces people to deliver, individual freedom no longer has any meaning. A workforce participation mandate is precisely what it appears to be: slavery. Slavery deprives a man of his most basic freedoms, therefore it cannot be coupled with the libertarian philosophy of the American Constitution. Since Rawls's theory of social justice eventually depends on a workforce mandate, his entire theory is at odds with the American founding.

From social justice to commodified liberty

In an effort to further integrate egalitarianism into the American constitutional republic, egalitarians attempt to redefine the term "liberty" in the same way they try to redefine "justice". Their method is simple: liberty is defined as social justice. Rawls makes this argument in two principles,[5] the first of which says that "each person participating in a practice, or affected by it, has an equal right to the most extensive liberty compatible with a like liberty for all".

Superficially, this sounds like the principle in the Declaration of Independence, namely that we are endowed with liberty by our Creator. If this were his point, he would essentially be on the same page as our Founders. However, that is not what Rawls says. The first point of his principle is "a like liberty for all", which means that everyone has the same amount—the same quantity—of liberty. While easily mistaken for an alternative expression of the principle from the Declaration, in reality this is the first step toward a quantification of liberty.

Rather than defining liberty as a God-given state of human existence, as America's Founding Fathers did, Rawls turns liberty into a commodity.

The second part of his definition of liberty brings him closer to completing the commodification of liberty. One man's liberty, he explains, must

---

5. See Rawls (1957, p. 654).

be "compatible" with the same liberty for everyone else. In other words, liberty has now become interpersonal.

This is a fundamental ideological change from how liberty is defined in the Declaration of Independence. There, liberty is individual, an endowment to each person from his Creator; it is never the case that one person is less free because of the liberty another person enjoys.

The only interpersonal aspect of liberty is that one man shall not restrict another man's liberty. A man's liberty is best guaranteed in the absence of other people's interference.

In the Rawlsian definition, however, the interpersonal relationship is essential: one man's liberty is contingent upon the liberty of others. If one man enjoys less liberty, it is because another man has more of it. Therefore, liberty is a distributional matter—a commodity to be distributed among individuals—whereupon it also becomes political. Every matter that is political, is a matter for state involvement in the lives of individual citizens.

Rawls never explains why the commodity of liberty is not available in such abundance that every man can enjoy it in full. He assumes that it is limited in quantity, i.e., scarce to the point where its distribution necessarily becomes a political matter.

By contrast, the Declaration of Independence explains that we are all equally endowed with liberty by the very virtue of having been created in God's image. Liberty is equal to all of us and it is individual such that one man's liberty does not depend on the liberty of any other man. It is a property inherent to every man. We all start our lives with that liberty; it is not something we have to acquire. It is given to all of us in equal amount, and not by government—but by God.

Rawls, on the other hand, necessitates an active process of acquisition of liberty. Since it is limited in quantity, and since one man's quantity of liberty is contingent upon the quantity held by everyone else, his liberty also comes at the expense of the liberty of others. The practical meaning of this is that liberty, according to egalitarians, is not endowed, but acquired in either of two ways: interaction between individuals where they compete for the commodity of liberty; or through redistribution by government.

Since Rawls makes clear that one man shall not have more liberty than any other man, he necessitates government involvement for the purposes of redistribution. In practice, this means that his ideology, egalitarianism, originates liberty in government. The Declaration of Independence, by contrast, originates liberty in God.

Rawls commodifies liberty because he needs it to fit it into his theory of social justice. Since social justice can only prevail by the hand of government, a man's liberty depends directly on the extent to which government intervenes in his life—and in the lives of his fellow citizens. According to the egalitarian ideology and social justice, its political practice, it is only through government that a man's freedom can be guaranteed.

The Declaration of Independence explains that all men are born equally endowed with a full amount of liberty. The Constitution, including the 14th Amendment, reinforces our equality as defined in the Declaration. Egalitarians ignore the Founders' definition of liberty as an endowment directly from God. Instead, by commodifying liberty,

a) They secularize liberty by originating it with government;

b) They tie liberty to social justice, making government responsible for actively providing every man with an equal amount; and

c) They mandate redistribution by government in order to end the inequality of liberty.

From commodified liberty to the welfare state

Already in his first egalitarian writings, Rawls acknowledged that when liberty is commodified, and when government is responsible for distributing it, government will need some form of measurement of liberty (1957, 654). Bluntly, liberty must be measurable from less to more.[6] The possession of liberty must therefore be directly visible in the form of the possession of some tangible asset, commonly divisible among all people. This asset could be "utility", i.e., a basic positive experience of having one's needs and wants satisfied. Rawls's theory of social justice relies on utilitarianism in its practice, but utility is a difficult entity to measure. Therefore, the commodification of liberty inevitably lands in money. It is the preferred measurement of commodified liberty in particular because it greatly facilitates government intervention in the distribution of liberty among the citizenry.

To turn Rawls's theory of social justice into practice, the first question one needs to answer is: what part of a man's possessions—again translated into monetary value—is relevant to the measurement of his liberty?

---

6. British philosopher H.L.A. Hart notes that Rawls only allows for "restriction of liberty for the sake of liberty itself" (1973, 537). However, this lexicographic ranking of liberty is not compatible with Rawls's claim that liberty can be "more" or "less".

There is only one answer to this question: all of it. A man's entire possessions that are quantifiable in money, are relevant. What is colloquially referred to as the "standard of living" becomes the base for not only measuring one man's liberty, but also comparing his liberty to that of others. Any restriction in what monetizable possessions should be used as measurement, will lead to arbitrary judgments; should the ownership of a pair of shoes be counted, but not a speedboat?

The problem with designing government policies based on interpersonal comparisons is that government cannot go from house to house and measure the actual value of all our material possessions. Therefore, government uses our income as a proxy; it is assumed that a man's standard of living is proportionate to his income. Therefore, a government that seeks to guarantee equal distribution of liberty based on Rawls's theory of social justice, will for practical purposes measure that distribution in the form of income. Those who earn less are entitled to more; those who earn more are obligated to give up some.

Without government intervention, Rawls presumes that individuals will try to hoard as much liberty as they can, indifferent to the consequences for others. By his theory, people are rational egoists whose personal maximization preferences clash with, and therefore exclude, compassion for others.[7] Therefore, if government does not intervene, some people will be less free than others.

The idea of progressive income taxation springs from this principle: by taking an increasingly large share of the earnings of high-income households, government slows down their ability to build wealth and raise their standard of living. A marginal tax rate that eventually reaches 100 percent will fall solidly in line with the ideological purpose behind social justice.

At the other end of the government budget, entitlements amend to lower incomes, adding cash as well as eligibility for various in-kind services. The latter category allows a person to spend his money elsewhere, indirectly increasing his income.

Eventually, egalitarian ideology prescribes that differences in standard of living be eradicated. This is the practical meaning behind Rawls's commodification of liberty. Every individual should enjoy the same income and consumption levels as everyone else. Since this is an ideological endeavor, it does not take into account how the welfare state changes economic incentives, with high taxes dissuading workforce participation and entitlements

---

7. See Bowie (1974), Schaar (1974).

encouraging idleness with work-free income. The goal is to reconfigure the relative economic relations between individuals, and thereby reconfigure the distribution of liberty across society as a whole. In order to reach that goal, the egalitarian must eventually have government's redistribution efforts span across the entire economy; the smaller the scope for private-sector economic activity, the easier it is—in theory—for government to secure absolute equality in economic resources and liberty.

3

From the Welfare State to Tyranny

WHEN LIBERTY IS QUANTIFIED, its value can be zero, as in a person having no income and no other economic resources. On the face of it, this makes sense: an enslaved person is deprived of his liberty. The Declaration of Independence says that a slave is endowed by our Creator with the same liberty as every other man, a right that was eventually extended to all Americans with the end of slavery. It was government that created legal slavery; after the Civil war government retreated from the invasion of individual liberty that was slavery. This retreat was in line with the ideological foundation of the U.S. constitutional republic as expressed in the Declaration of Independence. There is only one way to liberty for every individual, namely through the end of government incursions into people's lives.[1]

It is, in other words, a simple matter under American liberty to explain the meaning of zero liberty and provide its remedy. Rawls's theory of social justice does not lend itself to the same purpose as easily. While there is no doubt that egalitarians in general are as opposed to slavery as libertarians, their theory does not define slavery based on their concept of liberty. When liberty is commodified, as it is in Rawls's theory, the question

---

1. As noted earlier, as imperfect as the union was that our Founding Fathers created, it did end slavery within a century of its creation. The point here is not whether or not slavery existed at the founding of our constitutional republic; the point is that the philosophy upon which it was founded did not permit slavery. The journey to the end of that abhorrent practice was, obviously, too long, but it did happen and slavery was done away with. Without the values underpinning our founding documents, it is likely that slavery would have lived on far beyond the 1860s.

of a person's liberty is related strictly to his material possessions. If a person who is enslaved has access to food of the same quality as every other person in his society; if his living quarters are of the same standard; if all his other material possessions are of the same standard as those that free men have; then Rawls's theory cannot meaningfully define him as a slave. Absurdly, but consistently under his theory, Rawls cannot say that the slave has less liberty than an independent man.

This conclusion of social justice, which is inevitable from Rawls's theory, is not intended. However, a theory that leads to serious unintended consequences is still responsible for them, especially when proponents of that theory aspire to apply it in policy and legislation. Where libertarian theory squarely concludes that a man's liberty is contingent upon the containment and restriction of government, egalitarian theory concludes, with equal determination, that government must grow and secure that everyone enjoys the same amount of liberty. Once that is the case; once the material resources that quantify liberty have been evenly distributed; the egalitarian has created a free and just society. It is free and just regardless of the actual circumstances under which people live.

Forced labor

The slavery example demonstrates what this means in practice. By egalitarian standards, a man's liberty, even when minuscule, is morally acceptable if every one of his fellow citizens enjoy the exact same amount of liberty. Once the egalitarian has accomplished this equal distribution, his pursuit of liberty stops.

Under the ideology behind the American constitutional republic, the pursuit does not stop until every hindrance to liberty, for every person, has been removed. Liberty is entirely individual; one man's liberty does not restrict the liberty of others: liberty is not exchangeable or tradable. The only threat to a man's liberty (aside criminal acts) is by means of government action. Therefore, the only way to secure the liberty of any man—every man—is to remove the hindrances to his liberty that government has put in his path.

Under American liberty, government does not give us liberty; government inserts itself between us and liberty. Its expansion is immoral; its retreat is moral.

In a manner of speaking, the libertarian ideology considers liberty to be a given, an exogenous phenomenon to which we have to adjust the role of government. By contrast, under egalitarian ideology liberty is endogenous and contingent upon government action.

These opposing views of liberty contrast against how the two ideologies view prosperity. To the libertarian, prosperity is endogenous, the result of how society is organized. When individuals are given the proper conditions, they pursue and build prosperity. By contrast, the egalitarian thinks of prosperity as a given, an exogenous entity that is either justly or unjustly distributed among the citizenry.

Government is organized around either the protection of liberty, or the distribution of prosperity.

Egalitarianism assumes that a society compliant with its policy prescription in the form of social justice—elimination of all economic differences between individuals—will elevate the poor to more enjoyable heights of prosperity. The method for making this happen is economic redistribution by government, in other words the welfare state.

Problems arise when the tax base for the welfare state fails to deliver the resources necessary to fund the welfare state. The economic mechanisms that produce prosperity are not immune to the level of government involvement in the economy. The welfare state discourages productive economic activity, such as workforce participation, by providing entitlements unrelated to—even negatively correlated with—a person's income and productive efforts. Similarly, progressive taxation that increasingly reduces the reward of earning higher incomes, also discourage productive efforts as well as economic risk-taking.

The more redistributed taxes and entitlements are, the more they discourage economic growth. Over time, the pursuit of social justice thus weighs down the economy, slowly replacing growth in prosperity with economic stagnation.[2] Increasingly, tax revenue falls short of the entitlement spending that the welfare state needs to keep up in order to maintain social-justice compliant redistribution. Since an egalitarian government is not going to give up its pursuit of social justice, its only option over time is to gradually increase the tax burden on the private sector. As a result, the cost of government gradually rises to the point where it is unbearable for the private sector. As economic growth slows down and approaches standstill, economic stagnation is accepted by egalitarians, even elevated as a palatable price for social justice.[3]

---

2. For a statistical review, see Larson (2014).
3. Larson (2018, pp. 85–89).

When government expansion comes at the price of economic stagnation, one particular question arises: is there a limit to government expansion before all economic differences have been eradicated? Overall, the egalitarian literature leaves this question unanswered, and so does Rawls. The lack of comment on this issue begs another question: is social justice worth a ride to the end of the road to serfdom? There is, namely, no analytical or even theoretical point in egalitarian theory at which equally shared poverty becomes a greater moral problem than social justice is a virtue.

A third question arises: if equally shared poverty is a price worth paying for the fact that it is equally shared; if policies in pursuit of social justice can be justified even as they confine people to a life in material misery; then what other incursions into people's private life can be justified in the name of social justice?

Social justice decouples a person's access to food, shelter, clothes, health care, means of transportation and other necessities and amenities, from his workforce participation. Suppose that this leads to a collapse in the supply of necessary resources, from food to health care to infrastructure to education. With no incentives to work, people reduce their participation to a minimum while enjoying to a maximum the entitlements that government has provided them with.

Suppose, over time, the lack of workforce participation leads to a collapse in the supply of goods and services in general. Is it morally justifiable for government to mandate workforce participation?

The reason for a collapse in the supply of goods and services does not have to be long-term in nature. It may not even be caused by disincentives toward productive economic behavior. Social and economic unrest can arise even as people still put in productive efforts at work. As demonstrated by Venezuela during and after Hugo Chavez, a social and economic collapse can emerge by the very virtue of the pursuit of social justice. Lack of food leads to widespread malnutrition, lack of resources in health care cause unmitigated spread of diseases, while other systemic shortages severely infringe on basic human life.

Is it justifiable for government to coercively increase workforce participation in order to address disruptive supply shortages? Is it justifiable to force physicians to provide health care, under the penalty of jail time? Is it justifiable to force a farmer to work under equal threats of punishment under criminal law?

Forced labor, another term for slavery, is totalitarian by definition. It is unacceptable regardless of whether it applied to part of the population under the first 90 years of the American constitutional republic, or is state-imposed in a contemporary socialist country.

For egalitarians, the problem arises when slavery is introduced as a workforce participation mandate. The more broadly it applies, the closer society moves toward unabridged totalitarianism.

Does egalitarianism provide a clear barrier against the enslavement of a population in the name of social justice? Rawls does not ignore this question: he is at least somewhat aware that his theory of social justice can lend unintended support to tyranny. He appears to believe that his theory provides a bulwark of democracy against any totalitarian tendencies in a society. His theory mandates that all citizens be granted equal access to the institutions that affect their lives, such as the legislative functions. The assumption is that universal suffrage gives the majority sufficient means to keep totalitarianism at bay.

This is an understandable but ultimately false assumption: universal suffrage is necessary but not sufficient. So long as a society relies solely on the majority principle to guarantee every man's liberty, it is always one election away from its own repeal.

However, Rawls does not see the need for a firewall against totalitarianism to prevent forced labor. Since egalitarianism holds prosperity as exogenous—a given entity independent of the pursuit of social justice—there is no need in their theory for a political mechanism, or constitutional preemption, to ban forced labor. That does not mean egalitarians endorse it; they simply do not see a problem with it.

For this very reason, the question remains unanswered: can the pursuit of social justice be worth the enslavement of an entire population?

Another angle to the same problem is the fact that egalitarianism, especially as presented by Rawls, is built on the implicit premise that social justice is attainable, and maintainable, without any harm to prosperity. On the contrary, by means of universal suffrage, the pursuit of social justice is a sufficient means to keep a society from descending into tyranny.

Utilitarianism

There are three problems with Rawls's single-handed reliance on universal suffrage, in other words majority rule. First, the rejection of tyranny does not follow from the acceptance of social justice. It is a non-sequitur. Not only does the egalitarian definition of liberty leave the issue of totalitarianism unresolved, but eventually, as economic growth gives way to stagnation, it actually relies on a totalitarian measure to guarantee the equal distribution of liberty. That measure is mandatory workforce participation.

Secondly, there is the open question of what egalitarians will do if the majority rejects social justice. They could decide that it is in the best interest of everyone if everyone, on his own merits, were allowed to strive for whatever goal they have set for themselves, including trying to become the richest man in the country.

This possibility creates a conflict between universal suffrage and majority rule on the one hand, and social justice on the other. Rawls offers no solution; if he did, it would have to do one of two things:

1. Acknowledge that social justice as actual policy—what we know as the welfare state—stands and falls with an egalitarian legislative majority; when egalitarians lose, they concede and accept that another ideology will define the course of society; or

2. Elevate social justice above majority rule, in other words: tyranny.

Philosophically, Rawls works hard to remain on the side of democracy. Having made clear in his 1957 paper that liberty is akin to—if not identical with—money and material possessions, in his 1971 book *A Theory of Justice* he tries to walk back some of his theory. He states that liberty has a special status, that people should have "more" liberty before they have anything else in their lives. Ultimately, he cannot escape the fact that his definition of liberty does not include universal suffrage; that it is tagged on as a separate feature.

The third problem with Rawls's attempt to fit social justice and universal suffrage under one roof is that he himself allows for a trade-off between liberty and wealth.[4] This trade-off can continue ad infinitum, or at least until we are all equal in everything including poverty.[5]

To drive home his point about the supremacy of egalitarian redistribution over every other value, Rawls even wants to "nullify" economic differences caused by differences in "natural endowment".[6] As explained earlier, a good basketball player cannot be paid more than a mediocre player. Such

---

4. See Barry (1973), Lessnoff (1974).
5. See Daniels (1974).
6. See Bentley (1974), Daniels (1974), Goff (1983), Gorr (1983), Blaug (1986).

economic differences are, namely, unjust and, through its commodification, liberty distributed unequally.

A neutralization of natural endowments has far-reaching consequences, both for the ecomomy and for individual freedom. People's ability to stretch their talents is one of the most important factors behind economic growth. It leads to career development, growth in professional skills and productivity, and to entrepreneurship and risk taking. By decoupling productivity from economic reward, Rawls hampers growth in all these forms, but there is more: his argument against the tie between abilities and earnings extends to intellectual talents as well. By his own theory, Rawls cannot be permitted to earn more money from his impressive scholarly achievements—let alone his book sales—than a less productive professor.

In fact, Rawls cannot earn more than a man who chooses manual labor because he does not possess the intelligence that Rawls utilizes for his research and authorship.

This point is no more controversial than when Rawls's theory suggests that a tall and talented basketball player cannot make more money than a short, clumsy team mate. To detach the productive use of intelligence from reward is akin to eradicating the earnings differences between a highly skilled surgeon and one of poor skills.

Rawls's theory of social justice is fundamentalist in its emphasis on economic redistribution. Rawls himself inserts qualifications and never discusses economic redistribution to any greater extent. However, he takes his theory far enough that liberty is equated with social justice, and social justice is equated with economic redistribution; a society cannot be socially just and its citizens cannot live in liberty unless all economic differences between individual citizens have been eradicated.

Nobel Prize Laureate, economist Kenneth Arrow provides a window to just how radical and potentially totalitarian Rawls's theory actually is. He generalizes the commodification of liberty by noting the similarity between Rawls's definition of liberty and what economists call "utility"; liberty has no meaning beyond the material experiences that yield "utility".

A practical, and highly pertinent problem arises. Who is to determine utility experiences? From the policy maker's viewpoint, seeking an answer to this question is necessary for the advancement of a social-justice agenda. If a legislature is going to successfully redistribute liberty between citizens, it needs a measurement of the entity to be redistributed—a measurement that is impartial between individuals. Money has this property: one person makes a certain amount of money, another makes a different amount. Redistribution is successful when the two sums of money are equal.

If the measurement is utility, a different problem arises. It is similar in nature, but it is perhaps even more invasive from the viewpoint of individual freedom. It is already established that Rawls's definition of liberty is material and interpersonal in nature. Therefore, to compare it interpersonally, government would need to translate liberty into a unit, not only common to all individuals but also measurable independently of all individuals. As Kenneth Arrow suggests, that measurement could be utility.

As an example of the consequences of this translation of liberty into utility, consider the distribution of health care—a material resource befitting Rawls's liberty definition—in countries with single-payer health care. The decisions on who shall be treated and who shall not, are made by a government entity, often a board of health experts, based on one form or another of utility estimates. The common formula is known as Quality Adjusted Life Years (QALY). It is used, e.g., in Britain, where the National Health Service covers almost the entire population. The distribution of health care resources—work hours, health care facilities and medical supplies—are decided based on guidelines from the National Institute for Health and Clinical Excellence (NICE). To determine what patients get treatment and what patients do not, NICE applies QALY and thereby determines what improvements in quality of life a patient will experience from any given medical procedure.

It is not the patient who determines the improvement—it is the government body. This has a profound meaning for individuals seeking health care, especially since the British government (through its health-care agency) has established a cost cap for medical procedures. The cost cap is then divided by the number of quality-adjusted life years that the procedure is expected to gain. The bottom line—the money vs. the improvement in quality of life that government expects a person to experience—then decides what patients are treated and for what.

Since health care is strictly rationed, those decisions also mean that government decides who does not get his health conditions treated. When utility-based calculations are used to distribute health care, individual patients lose control over their own medical treatment; their own experiences of health are replaced with impartial, interpersonal calculations by the government that has been charged with distributing health care.

Since the Rawlsian definition of liberty equates material resources such as health care with liberty, this means that with regard to health care, people lose control over their own liberty. Ultimately, this can lead to them losing control over their lives. If government estimates that the cost of a specific treatment exceeds the quality of life improvement that said government calculates, the patient is denied even life-saving treatment.

Explains Jane M Orient, executive director of the Association of American Physicians and Surgeons:[7]

> there is an unbridgeable chasm between life and death. Nevertheless, the discontinuity apparently escapes those who set up relative value scales based on "quality-adjusted life-years" (QALYs). The unstated assumption is that at some point on the QALY scale, visible to experts, the value of a life becomes negative—even less than the value of death.

If similar calculations are used on a general level, for the distribution of housing, clothing and food, at some point individual lives become entirely subordinate to the ideological pursuit of social justice.

If we maintain the distribution model for the material resources that constitute liberty, the egalitarian ideology can once again return to the question of mandatory labor. Thomas Scanlon, philosopher and Harvard professor emeritus, drives home this point:[8]

> A liberty in the sense in which Rawls uses the term is defined by a complex of rights along with the correlative duties of others to aid or not interfere.

On the face of it, Scanlon's observation seems to be little more than a technical note. However, the commodification of liberty means that when a person has the right to a resource—be it health care or food or any other—someone has an obligation to provide that resource. If government cannot summon the resource, its promise, and its pursuit of social justice, rings hollow.

By Scanlon's words, every man has a duty to provide for other people's liberty. This means a duty of active provision: a person must perform an act in order to provide for another man's liberty. The door is now open for government—ultimately the majority of the people—to coerce individuals into providing for the commodified liberty of others. This coercion is implied,

---

7. See Orient (2006).
8. See Scanlon (1973, p. 1035)

even prescribed, and unintentionally allows a combination of social justice and totalitarianism.

Rule by moral decree

Under universal suffrage, there is always the possibility that a majority votes to reject social justice for some other ideology. To secure a society in the image of social justice, Rawls develops a method for elevating egalitarianism above other ideologies. He suggests a method that will lead to the codification of social justice.

While Rawls does not explicitly say so, he hints of a process where a panel of government experts determine what moral principle shall underpin our society. This is done by the identification of "provisional expressions" or "premises" of a moral nature.[9] The expert panel elevates these premises to the standard of objective facts; since according to Rawls, it is government's duty to redistribute resources—including liberty—among the citizenry, it is also government's duty to protect and even enforce the theory that lends moral legitimacy to economic redistribution.

Even though the point with a panel of moral experts would be to elevate the theory of social justice to something akin to scientific truth, that is not possible. The standards of evidence in the natural sciences are far too rigorous, and the study of ideologies and moral values was never intended to rise to those standards in the first place. Bluntly, one cannot go out and point to moral principles and determine their existence. At best, we can investigate what moral principles people live by, but that is only a descriptive form of evidence. A panel of moral experts would want to establish prescriptive evidence elevating one ideology above others.[10] Yet that is essentially what Rawls is striving for. He wants his egalitarian ideology to:

---

9. See Worland (1973).

10. Rawls aspires to rise above the debate over what justice is. As noted by McCoy (1973), if Rawls has indeed produced such a theory, it would be comparable—but not equal—in scientific status to laws of nature. The difference, McCoy explains (p. 352),

> is that the physicist is dealing with actions of inanimate objects, so that his theory must account for all observable instances; if it does not, there is a defect or inadequacy in the theory. Since our judgments of justice are the product of choice, and since the human is eminently capable of inconsistency, Rawls can use his abstract characterization of a person's general body of judgments to pronounce one or more of their choices inconsistent with the others.

He then suggests as a test of the validity of Rawls's theory that a person can be

a) Have empirical status, in other words, "exists", and at the same time

b) Be prescriptive, in other words tells us what "ought to exist".[11]

It would be the task of a panel of moral experts to validate egalitarianism. In other words, government takes it upon itself to establish the founding moral principle of society. However, in doing so, government also decides what moral principles are not acceptable. Under American liberty, there can be no such role for government. The principles of the American constitutional republic stipulate our duty to not interfere with people's liberty; we accept that they live by their own moral principles under one common moral denominator, i.e., respect for the sovereignty of the individual:

- One person can live by the moral principle that he ought to share everything he makes with as many people as possible;
- Another person may live by the principle that he shall not share any of his property with anyone, ever.

They are both perfectly free to live under their moral guideline of choice, and to dispose of their income, their wealth and their time as they please. The only restriction is to never violate the life, liberty or property of another person. This includes a ban on imposing mandates on an individual or group to dispose of their time and property as per the demands of others.

It deserves to be pointed out that the co-existence of mutually incompatible moral values is not evidence of a nihilistic society. The fact that one person refuses to be altruistic and charitable, while another chooses to be, does not mean that I condone both behaviors, nor does it mean that the majority of people are indifferent to both. All it means is that each individual citizen can choose with whom to socialize, and with whom to have economic relations.

Suppose a business owner refuses to donate money to charities that benefit people of a different faith than his. Suppose one of his competitors donates to all kinds of charities. Which one do I choose to spend my money at? The second one, simply because I disagree with the moral values of the first business owner. I do not have a moral duty to benefit him with my

---

convinced to change his mind in judgments on justice if it can be "persuasively demonstrated" to that person that his judgments are inconsistent.

11. See McCoy (1973).

money, nor do I have a moral right to force him to donate to charities he does not approve of.

A nihilistic society is a society where people are indifferent to right and wrong. A free society is one where people can express their preferences for right and wrong without interfering with the liberty of others to do the same.

A totalitarian society is where people impose their moral values on others by means of government coercion. Here again, egalitarianism opens a channel to a totalitarian society. Egalitarianism cannot co-exist with other ideologies. Only one moral principle can be allowed to define the interaction between individuals. That principle, says Rawls, is the elimination of economic differences between individuals, namely the complete reconfiguration of society in the image of social justice.

Rawls does not believe, namely, that people will voluntarily participate in charitable causes. He assumes instead that people in general are so-called rational egoists.[12] With this assumption, he creates a space for his theory that would otherwise not exist. Since his egalitarianism demands far-reaching economic redistribution, and since the practice of that redistribution demands the creation and perpetuation of a welfare state, all the efforts behind that ideological edifice would be in vain if people simply were charitable by nature and upbringing.

The presumption of egoism is not just of theoretical interest. It is integrated into the entire process that, according to Rawls, will establish the moral principles of a society. When his panel of moral experts meets to figure out what morality "there is", they will do so with the presumption of egoism as a starting point. Thereby, their obvious conclusion will be that society needs coerced redistribution.

At this point, Rawls's egalitarianism once again runs up against the chasm of tyranny. By presuming that people are egoists, Rawls creates an inherent conflict between his panel of moral experts and universal suffrage. If people vote against forced redistribution, egalitarians can claim that they do so because they are egoists, not because they prefer individual freedom. Since egoism is generally considered to be morally inferior to egalitarianism, a majority vote to reject economic redistribution becomes a pretext for the termination of democracy and the enforcement of egalitarianism by government decree.

---

12. See Bowie (1974), Schaar (1974).

4

Foundations of American Liberty

Philosopher and Harvard professor Robert Nozick once asked[1]: "If the state did not exist would it be necessary to invent it?" He also pointed in the opposite direction, asking: "Why not have anarchy?"

The two questions put a compelling framework around the American Constitution. The Founders saw it necessary to have a government, a state, but it was equally necessary for them to limit its powers and duties. It was, they thought, necessary to invent the state but equally necessary to invent the method of constitutionally enumerating its powers.

To start from the bottom, the question of anarchy is summarily dismissed by Rawls, who sees anarchy as a state of chaos and conflict. This is understandable given his assumption that man is a "rational egoist". An egoist is a person who pursues his goals and needs with indifference to any harm he causes others as a result of his actions. Logically, in a world full of egoists, only government can guarantee safety, security—and that everyone gets what he needs. If egoism is in human nature, nobody will care for the poor. Without a welfare state people will refuse to help those who suffer.

Nozick starts with an entirely different outlook on humanity. His question, whether or not it would be necessary to invent the state, guides him to an entirely different conclusion about government. His libertarian theory of justice starts with a[2]

> nonstate situation in which people generally satisfy moral constraints and generally act as they ought. Such an assumption is not

---

1. See Nozick (1974, p. 3).
2. See Nozick (1974, p. 5).

wildly optimistic; it does not assume that all people act exactly as they should. Yet this state-of-nature situation is the best anarchic situation one could reasonably hope for.

He then proposes a test for whether or not the state is indeed necessary. If it can be made credible, he explains, that a society without a state—without government—is improved by the introduction of government, then government has been proven to be a necessity.

The next question is what role the state should play in people's lives. Egalitarian ideology turns that question on its head, asking instead what role the individual should play under the state. If man by nature is an egoist, the state needs to fold the individual into a societal master plan guided by non-egoistic moral principles. If, on the other hand, man is an altruist or at least generally compassionate; in other words, if he is adverse to others suffering as a result of his actions; then the state should play a subordinate role to the individual.

If we limit our inquiry into the competing ideologies of egalitarianism and libertarianism to the relationship between the state and the individual, and if that limited inquiry is based on no deeper understanding of the individual than a contrast between egoism and compassion, then all we have are two different ideas of human nature. We have the egalitarian view, a dystopian theory where man is a rational egoist; we also have the libertarian view, a more optimistic theory where people are compassionate and "generally satisfy moral constraints".

At this point, two theories of human nature contrast with one another like two axioms elevated beyond the pursuit of proof. Therefore, they are equally valid.[3] However, there is a tie breaker: God.

Intuitively, God's role in human life and human society is apparent. Philosophically, the key to His relevance is Rawls's idea that man is an egoist by nature. That is not the case: God is not an egoist. He is not indifferent to human suffering, and since man is His creation, neither are we.

At the same time, the fact that human nature is not egoistic does not mean it is altruistic; absence of one extreme does not imply the presence of its opposite. God has equipped us with both compassion and self interest, a combination that generally keeps us from becoming egoists. However, this combination also creates a conflict in human nature, a conflict that helps us answer Nozick's two questions about anarchy and the state.

---

3. See Gill (1976).

The best way to understand this conflict is to distinguish between egoism and self interest. We are self-interested in that we strive to better our own lives and the lives of those we are responsible for. We pursue happiness according to our own preferences, but unlike the egoist, our self interest compels us to see the suffering of others, especially as a consequence of our own actions.

The human existence is one of striking the right balance between self interest and compassion. That is not to say egoism and other harmful behavior do not exist; as Nozick observes, we can generalize about human nature, but never universalize. We mostly, but not always, act "as we should", in other words, in our own interest but on the right side of egoism.

While self interest is the active consideration of consequences of one's own actions, compassion is the consideration of suffering independent of one's own actions. A person drifting more toward self interest will have a narrower perception of human suffering in general; a more compassionate person will be less inclined to act in his own self interest. By striving to balance the two, we generally uphold the moral principles that constitute and maintain a society without government.

The state is invented in order to prevent harmful consequences of exceptional behavior; the question is: how big a state do we need?

The individual and the minimal state

With his two questions, Nozick suggests that liberty is jeopardized in either of two ways: descent into anarchy or ascent into tyranny. The path in either direction depends on the relation between, on the one hand, the individual and the state and, on the other hand, the policies that the state uses to protect or affect that relationship. We refer to those policies as "public policy".

In their design of the federal government, the authors of our Constitution were careful to restrict the state, not the individual. This approach defined the relationship they created between the people and the state. They preferred elected representatives to political parties and a constitutional republic to a parliamentary system. They also elevated the individual above government, as visible in, e.g., the Tenth Amendment.

By the same token, Nozick sees government as an enumerated residual to human nature (p. 11):

> Only after the full resources of the state of nature are brought into play, namely all those voluntary arrangements and arrangements

persons might reach acting within their rights, and only after the effects of these are estimated, will we be in a position to see how serious are the inconveniencies that yet remain to be remedied by the state, and to estimate whether the remedy is worse than the disease.

There is a clear path from this libertarian faith in human nature back to the Bible. When the Israelites no longer believed they were able to live in full morality and harmony, they asked for a state—judges—to make sure that disputes, be it over property or harm to a person, would not result in the exaction of over-compensation.[4]

Resolution of disputes is an enumerated power. The relationship between the individual and the state ranks the individual above the state; the state is residual to the individual. Our Constitution does the same: the Founders understood human nature deep enough to know that a state was necessary, but that this state must be restricted and confined to a limited set of duties and powers.

In defining the relationship between government and the people, the Founders applied the Biblical understanding of what motivates human action. This understanding consists of two dimensions, the first of which is that between self-interest and compassion. This is the dimension that motivates our actions.

The second dimension is that between reason and passion. It is the interactive dimension. Reason is a man's ability to make dispassionate decisions, uncoupled from his self-motivating dimension; passion is decision-making while being guided primarily by one's self motivation:

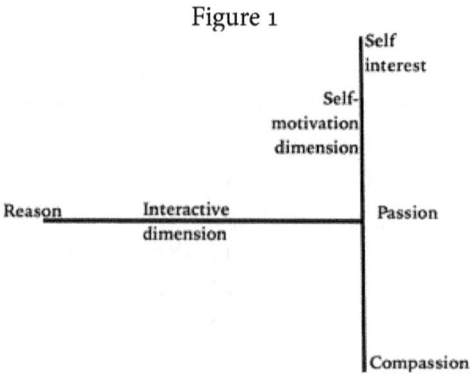

Figure 1

4. Judg. 2:11–18

Having understood the importance of dispassionate decision-making, the Israelites sought to prevent passion from taking over in conflict resolution.[5] Initially, that was also all the government they asked for. In a similar effort to limit the state, our Founding Fathers created a government with enumerated powers and separated branches. Likewise, Robert Nozick refers to the state that channels reason but curbs passion as the minimal state. Its powers are strictly enumerated: to protect life, liberty and property, and to be the arbiter of disputes.

Recognizing the tension between reason and passion, Nozick explains that:[6]

> private and personal enforcement of one's rights (including those rights that are violated when one is excessively punished) leads to feuds, to an endless series of acts of retaliation and exactions of compensation. And there is no firm way to settle such a dispute, to end it and to have both parties know it is ended.

In a society where exaction of compensation is governed more by emotional self interest than dispassionate judgment, the outcomes of conflict will gradually deprive people of their liberty and property. This creates a slippery slope on which a functioning society slowly deteriorates into anarchy. Once in anarchy, where no rules apply except brute force, he who is the biggest bully will eventually establish himself as a tyrant.

In short: where exaction of compensation is governed by passion instead of reason, eventually there will be no functioning society.

Nozick's minimal state is based on this recognition of human nature. It is, he says, the smallest tolerable state, a state confined to conflict resolution and the protection of life, liberty and property.[7] From a Christian perspective, the minimal state is also motivated by human nature, but with a slightly different angle to it. Reasoning themselves to the necessity of a minimal state, free and independent men will lead a better life with it than without it.

That is not to say human nature and the minimal state will coexist in uninterrupted harmony. From a Christian perspective, responsible citizenship is as necessary as it is challenging. The Bible provides ample insight into the complexities of human society, and the responsibilities we bear

---

5. "In those days there was no king in Israel, but every man did that which was right in his own eyes." (Judg. 17:6)
6. See Nozick (1974, p. 11).
7. See Nozick (1974, pp. 12–17; 26–27).

in order to preserve liberty. In the story of the Israelites under the judges, society repeatedly bounces up against its moral boundaries, but initially, thanks to a shared sense of responsibility, those boundaries hold firm.

The society that America's Founding Fathers had in mind was similar: they had no illusions about a society in perfect harmony. It would be a society where men could govern themselves by their own consent, provided that reason prevailed over passion. Imperfect but benevolent men, who generally abide by moral constraints, have at their disposal a state and its institutions that enhance their abilities to govern themselves. The institutions of government are limited to allow, as Nozick put it earlier, "voluntary arrangements" to meet both self-interested and compassionate needs. These arrangements are protected by judges—an impartial judiciary.

Herein lies the answer to Nozick's initial question: "If the state did not exist would it be necessary to invent it?" Yes: the minimal state, and only the minimal state.

Libertarianism vs. Objectivism

In its mission to protect life, liberty and property, the minimal state is concentrated entirely on protecting private life. Public life, i.e., interpersonal relations are the matter of voluntary agreements between individuals; the only role the state can play is in conflict resolution.

By contrast, the welfare state, in its implementation of social justice, starts with redefining—even socializing—interpersonal relations. Its involvement in public life then aims to redefine the conditions for private life by means of altering the outcomes of interpersonal relations. In other words, what the minimal state leaves untampered with, the welfare state changes by means of economic redistribution.

In altering the outcomes of voluntary trade, the welfare state permits one, and only one, set of moral values among the citizenry. It does so because it—the state—does not accept the moral content of the outcomes in private interaction. Rawls provides a good example: he does not believe that voluntary exchange will be beneficial enough for the worst-off citizens. Presuming his own definition of "beneficial enough" is morally superior to whatever definitions individual citizens may have, Rawls also superimposes his moral preference of social justice not only on those who will pay for his economic redistribution, but also on those who actually are worse off than most others. Under social justice, it is of no consequence if a poor person prefers to work his way to a better life than to depend on government.

In other words, under the welfare state's moral principle of social justice, morality enters the end point of human interaction, including economic exchange in particular. It defines principles stipulating how economic resources be redistributed after they have already been distributed among individuals by means of voluntary exchange.

Under libertarianism and American liberty, morality enters society through private relationships. Specifically, in the economy morality manifests itself in voluntary, gainful exchange in the free market. If economic exchange—such as paid work or trade of goods and services for money—is voluntary, then the outcomes are morally acceptable.

That does not mean every individual will agree that it is moral; people may disagree with how the free markets have distributed income, wealth, goods and services. However, in a free society with a minimal state, every individual is free to alter the outcomes of his own voluntary participation in trade. He is free to give what he has to others, for whatever reason. The only restriction on his voluntary, charitable endeavor is that it remains voluntary; so long as he does not seek to impose his moral views on his fellow citizens; so long as he does not seek to forcefully alter the outcome of voluntary exchange that he is not part of; his redistributive moral preference is perfectly compliant with the preservation of a free society.

The minimal state keeps politics out of private life; the welfare state exists for the very purpose of politicizing private life. In fact, the only way that the ideology of social justice can be turned into actual policy is through the political invasion of private life. As an example of what it means in practice, Emily Gill, retired Caterpillar Professor of political science at Bradley University, suggests that although an individual is free to make choices under the minimal state (1976, 196), and although he may be free from coercion,

> he is not free *for* life according to his preferred choice. Individuals are free from external compulsion as Nozick defines it, but they remain unfree for activities unavailable within the choice environment, rendered impossible by the machinations of the invisible hand, or the enabling of which makes claims upon collective social action.

Gill's point is that wherever there is a gap between a man's preferred economic outcomes—choices—and what he can attain through voluntary exchange with others, that gap compels "collective social action", i.e., state intervention. The gap may be regarded as moral by individual citizens, including those who cannot obtain their preferred outcomes; they may see it as a virtue to better their lives through work, education and thrift. Yet under the realm of social justice, their preferences are irrelevant: like Rawls, Gill imposes her moral preference on the end results of voluntary trade and thereby nullifies the preferences of others.

It is important to note that the absence of a superimposed society-wide moral preference neither implies nor necessitates moral relativism. American liberty excludes collective social action, but that does not relieve individual citizens of collective moral duties. The Christian pillar of American liberty defines those duties in the form of responsible citizenship: while there can be no legal requirement on individuals to take personal responsibility for the furtherance of a free society, its perpetuation does depend on the willingness of individual citizens to strive for self-determination, shun egoism and strike a balance between self interest and compassion.

It is prudent, in fact, to consider responsible citizenship as the prime moral duty of every free individual. To this point, there is a stern Biblical account of what happens when citizens shy away from responsible citizenship. God paints in stark colors the line between its virtues and the vices of its abandonment. On the one hand, man shall "study to be quiet, and to do your own business, and to work with your own hands."[8] In other words, the core virtue of individual responsibility is for each man to provide for himself and his loved ones.

On the other hand:[9]

> if any provide not for his own, and especially for those of his own house, he hath denied the faith and is worse than an infidel.

When a man ceases to uphold the virtue of self-determination, his character is in decline:[10]

> And withal they learn to be idle, wandering about from house to house; and not only idle, but tattlers also and busybodies, speaking things which they ought not.

This sounds as though, under the minimal state, people who fall on hardship would be left to fend for themselves. That is not the case—in fact,

---

8. 1. Thess. 4:4–7; 1. Thess. 4:11
9. 1. Tim. 5:8
10. 1. Tim. 5:13

the idea of abandoning those in need is shared between two authoritarian ideologies: fascism and objectivism. Unlike libertarianism, which is based on Christian ethics, these two ideologies rely on the discarding of what are considered as "weaker" individuals.

A good example illustrating the difference is the debate over austerity-driven spending cuts in a recession. Since the United States has never experienced an austerity episode, the nearest comparable example is Europe immediately after the 2008–10 Great Recession.

During this period, the primary (though not only) targets of austerity policies were Greece and Spain. The Greek parliament passed spending cuts with legislative lightning speed. In the first three years, 2009–12, total social-protection spending declined 4.9 percent, followed by another 11.2 percent, from 2012 to 2016.

For comparison, there have never been cuts in U.S. federal social-protection spending.

The Greek government was widely criticized for its austerity cuts. Government had built a welfare state in the image of social justice, with long-term promises of benefits around which people planned their personal finances. When the Greek government started walking back on its promises, many Greeks understandably got upset. The fact that those promises were excessive in the first place is a topic for another conversation; once the promises—entitlement programs—are in place, people will expect to be able to rely on them, especially in recessions. Their own finances, depleted by taxes and otherwise adjusted to the welfare state's vows of handouts, will not be of much help.

Public reactions to the immorality of austerity policies were for the most part negative, but some people with purported libertarian leanings suggested otherwise. In an essay for the Cobden Centre, economics professor Phillip Bagus of the King Juan Carlos University in Spain, praised austerity policies, in Greece as well as in Spain:[11]

> austerity is the necessary condition for recovery in Spain, the Eurozone, and elsewhere. The reduction of government spending makes real resources available for the private sector that formerly had been absorbed by the state. Reducing government spending makes profitable new private investment projects and saves old ones from bankruptcy.

---

11. See: http://www.cobdencentre.org/2012/11/the-myth-of-austerity/

There is an economics debate to be had over this argument, one that contrasts Austrian economic theory to original Keynesianism. That debate is for another forum, with one exception: if professor Bagus were correct that the economy benefits from being starved, then Greece and Spain should have recovered quickly from the crisis. That did not happen: as of 2017, the Greek economy had not shown any recovery from the depression-style crisis. The country's GDP was still 25 percent smaller than it was ten years earlier (adjusted for inflation).

To dismiss the destruction of one quarter of a country's economy as a necessity, is to dismiss monumental human suffering and reducing it to a policy instrument. It is, in other words, to rank the state above the individual. This happens by default under social justice, as a welfare state exists to rearrange private lives and private relations to its ideological liking. However, it does not mean that the abandonment of people, because the welfare state cannot pay its bills, is morally acceptable.

Professor Bagus's indifference to the effects of austerity was echoed by Gary Johnson, former Governor of New Mexico, during his 2012 bid for president. As a candidate for the Libertarian party, Johnson vowed to "propose to cut $1.4 trillion from the 2014 budget - 43 percent of the federal budget" with an equal share being cut from the defense budget.[12]

Johnson never stated how fast he would execute his cuts, and in his defense he did not propose those cuts as a way to balance the federal budget in a recession. It was simply a matter of principle. Yet in order to be credible—and moral—about his proposed cuts, Johnson would have to explain what he was going to cut from the budget, when and how.

The last part is of paramount importance: if budget cuts are made simply as a matter of ideological principle, with no regard to their human consequences, then Johnson's proposal collapses into pure objectivism. That, in turn, is an ideology whose foremost character trait is to Darwinianly leave the poor, weak and suffering by the moral wayside. In July 2017, Ayn Rand Institute board member Harry Binswanger demonstrated the practical meaning of this, as he attacked those who have become dependent on Obamacare for their health insurance.

Binswanger's context for the attack was a connection between two episodes of Republican ideological failure, the second one being the attempt in 2017 by the Congressional Republican majority to repeal Obamacare:[13]

12. See https://www.cbsnews.com/news/gary-johnson-compares-us-to-greece-laughs-at-obamas-economic-plan/

13. See Binswanger (2017).

An earlier instance was the Gingrich-led "Republican revolution" of 1995. The American people had swept in a Republican majority in Congress, because they liked Gingrich's "Contract with America," which called for some heavy-duty reining-in of government power and looting. President Clinton was "triangulating"—that is, capitulating to the Republicans. But two words from the intellectual establishment stopped the movement: "mean-spirited." ... This time, there is no two-word package, but it's the same idea" Any rollback of parasitism hurts the parasites. Parasites will be unable to suck blood. Unthinkable.

The political theory behind objectivism, as expressed in Binswanger's reference to people as "parasites" for depending on government, is the same as in the egalitarian ideology of social justice. Government shall make changes to society with indifference to the individual consequences of those changes. Just as Rawls's theory of social justice prescribes an expansion of government to achieve a certain socio-economic architecture—perfect economic redistribution—objectivism prescribes a contraction of government for similar purposes, and based on a similar principle regarding the state-individual relationship. The individual is an instrument for the goals of the state.

Reforms to the welfare state must follow the same ethical rules as charity. Under the minimal state, it is the moral duty of responsible citizens to help individuals in need. By the same token, under the welfare state it is the moral duty of government to provide for those to whom it has made entitlement promises. However, the welfare state inevitably fails to honor its promises,[14] and when it does, it is the state's moral duty to provide a path to self sufficiency for those to whom the welfare state can no longer deliver on its promises.

Charity as a moral obligation

There is considerable temptation in ideologies that put the state above the individual. Some men are attracted to the power that a well-filled government bank account commands, especially when large numbers of their fellow citizens become dependent on that money. Others find entitlement dependency appealing because it allows them to combine idleness with a full fridge.

14. Larson (2014) provides numerous examples from across Europe of how a fiscal crisis has led to sustained, major cuts in government spending.

Since the combination of these two paths to statism is formidable, the exercise of responsible citizenship is paramount for the protection and perpetuation of a free society. Among its virtues is to strike a balance between charity and able-bodied work ethic. This balance is the result of every man's struggle to balance self interest against compassion. Self interest drives men to be productive; compassion drives them to be charitable, to lift up those who have fallen on hard times.

The balance shifts over time: when self interest dominates, we tend to apply a narrow definition of "hard times" to those who cannot provide for themselves. When compassion dominates, the demands weaken on the able-bodied to provide for themselves.

The liberty that Nozick argues for within the realms of libertarianism allows men to strike this very balance. However, it is in the Bible that the personal conduct is defined, that leads to a balance between self interest and charity. The importance of the latter cannot be overstated:[15]

> Though I speak with the tongues of men and of angels, and have not charity, I am become as sounding brass, or a tinking cymbal. And though I have the gift of prophecy, and understand all mysteries, and all knowledge; and though I have all faith, so that I could remove mountains, and have not charity, I am nothing. And though I bestow all my goods to feed the poor, and though I give my body to be burned, and have not charity, it profiteth me nothing. Charity suffereth long, and is kind; charity envieth not; charity vaunteth not itself, is not puffed up.

In his second epistle, Peter emphasizes the virtuousness of charity:[16]

> Whereby are given unto us exceeding great and precious promises: that by these ye might be partakers of the divine nature, having escaped the corruption that is in the world through lust. And beside this, giving all diligence, add to your faith virtue; and to virtue knowledge; And to knowledge temperance; and to temperance patience; and to patience godliness; And to godliness brotherly kindness; and to brotherly kindness charity.

This moral obligation is one side of the charity coin. The other side is an equally strong moral imperative that charity is not a right:[17]

---

15. 1. Cor. 13:1–10
16. 2 Peter 1:4–7
17. 2. Thess. 3:7–10

> For yourselves know how ye ought to follow us: for we behaved not ourselves disorderly among you; Neither did we eat any man's bread for nought; but wrought with labour and travail night and day, that we might not be chargeable to any of you: Not because we have not power, but to make ourselves an ensample unto you to follow us. For even when we were with you, this we commanded you, that if any would not work, neither should he eat.

The purpose here is to reserve charity for those who are unable to provide for themselves. Likewise, the purpose is to ask of able-bodied men for work before reward.

Explains Paul in his Epistle to Titus:[18]

> But speak thou the things which become sound doctrine: That the aged men be sober, grave, temperate, sound in faith, in charity, in patience. The aged women likewise, that they be in behavior as becometh holiness, not false accusers, not given to much wine, teachers of good things; That they may teach the young women to be sober, to love their husbands, to love their children

Responsible citizenship is not only about protecting free society, but also about perpetuating it. In other words, the younger generations need to inherit its virtues:[19]

> Young men be likewise exhort to be sober minded. In all things shewing thyself a pattern of good works: in doctrine shewing uncorruptness, gravity, sincerity, Sound speech, that cannot be condemned; that he that is of the contrary part may be ashamed, having no evil thing to say of you.

It is virtuous to treat those in true need as truly deserving of charitable help.[20] A firm demarcation line between true need and self determination, and an equally firm commitment to those in true need, will preserve the state within its minimal confinements. When men demand good work ethic of each other, but fail to commit to charity, the limitations of the minimal state eventually break down.

---

18. Titus 2:1–4
19. Titus 2:6–8
20. 1. Tim. 5:1–5

5

Corruption of the Social Fabric

The exercise of responsible citizenship creates a social fabric of relationships, institutions, habits and culture that synchronize into societal stability. This stability is essential for liberty and prosperity; wherever there is a breakdown in the stability of society and the economy, poverty and tyranny flourish.

A society where the individual ranks above the state is also a society where the social fabric evolves organically through the interaction of free, independent men. Combining their self interest with compassion for others, they build a socio-economic environment where they can make economic decisions, interact and trade, and generally plan for the future. They can do so knowing that the payoff from whatever investments they make, in economic capital or social relations, will depend predominantly on their own decisions and actions.

By contrast, the absence of a reliable social fabric makes our future uncertain. Risk aversion drives people to shorten their horizon on investments, both in economic capital and in relationships. Short-sightedness gives priority to immediate self interest over other considerations; charity suffers, as does long-term economic commitment.

When a high-risk environment forces people to put charity aside, social tensions arise. The price that people pay for economic hardship increases exponentially—first from the crisis itself, which deprives people of jobs and ruins entrepreneurial endeavors, then by taking a toll on charity. That is not to say charity is entirely abandoned in hard times; there are many examples throughout history when communities have banded together to share what sparse resources they had, in order to survive together. The point is, instead, that self interest comes to guide the extension of charity. To paraphrase an Egyptian saying: when there is not enough to help both my cousin and the stranger, I prioritize to help my cousin and abandon the stranger; when there is not enough to help both my cousin and my brother, I prioritize my brother.

Such priorities are not morally acceptable—they are understandable. A society, a family, an individual in survival mode will narrow their scope and leave others to fend for themselves out of sheer, naked necessity. However, the very knowledge of what hard times means has been enough for human societies around the world to build private, voluntary support systems to prevent bad times from tearing at their very social fabric. Churches have played a crucial role in this endeavor, as have other voluntary organizations.

It is always easier for a community than for the state to handle an economic crisis and respond to the hardship that comes with it. The only exception to this rule is a full-scale depression of the kind the world endured in the 1930s. However, the help that the state can provide under such circumstances is not of the kind often associated with Keynesian economics, i.e., more permanent government spending. The help is instead aimed to reassure private maintenance of the social fabric, a help to self-help function that has no role under any other circumstances than an exceptionally deep crisis.

If the state takes any other role in relation to the social fabric, its contributions will be destructive.

Politicizing private life

A minimal state explicitly refrains from taking active responsibility for the social fabric. It provides a foundation of protection of life, liberty and property, enabling individual citizens to build their lives and their communities as they see fit. The functions of the minimal state make it possible for people to plan their lives with a long time horizon in mind. All other things equal, the more reliable the minimal state is in its protective role, the further into the future people can plan their lives.

Long-term stability in the state, and long-term predictability in private lives and relations, combine into an essential vehicle for prosperity. Entrepreneurs can invest with long-term return in mind, as opposed to quick profits; talented people can invest several years in education, being confident that once they graduate, they will be able to put their skills, talents and work ethic to good use. The rise of the American republic in her first two centuries, and her prevalence through the past 50 years, are attributable to the stability that a small but reliable government provides for the free economy.

The growth in government, federal, state and local, since the mid-20th century has thus far not substantially altered the stabilizing role that the state can provide. The American economy has not been as dynamic since then, with a notable but not disastrous slowdown in growth in the new millennium. However, for every new role that government takes on in private life, it jeopardizes the very stability and predictability that have contributed so substantially to making the American economy what it is today.

For every new role of government in private life, it expands its responsibility for maintaining the social fabric. Eventually, this has catastrophic consequences; many countries have experienced what it means when government fails to provide what it has promised. In recent years, the Greek economic crisis has come to represent these consequences. When a drastic macroeconomic downturn deprived government of large amounts of tax revenue, it was forced to make substantial cuts into entitlement programs under the welfare state. Drastic hardship followed, with widespread, abject poverty and sustained youth unemployment in excess of 50 percent. Some benefits for poor families were cut by 90 percent, others made pointless through crippling spending reductions.

Millions of Greeks had planned their everyday lives around the promises of benefits from government. They, in turn, built their interaction with others—especially economically—on those promises. Instead of saving money for health care needs, they relied on tax-paid medical services to be available as needed. Instead of saving substantial amounts of money for contingencies, they relied on welfare programs and unemployment insurance to pay out benefits as needed.

As the economic crisis hit Greece in 2008 and 2009, government embarked on a journey of austerity that, to date, is still ongoing. Its effects on Greek society have been catastrophic, in part because it has ripped into the very social fabric that keeps society stable, predictable and harmonious. Severe cuts in government spending and destructive increases in taxes have disrupted business relations and family budgets as well as investment plans and private plans for the future.

When government rapidly walks back on its promises, such as to be the sole provider of health care under a single-payer system, there are ripple effects in many different directions throughout society. When government walks back on its promises in many different parts of society, the ripple effects multiply, as do their consequences. In Greece, this has led to an economic and social devaluation of the entire country. Despite courageous efforts by the Greek people to keep their country in dignified shape, as of 2018 its current-price GDP had not yet returned to where it was fifteen years earlier. A wealth of economic gains, of proceeds from long-term commitments by investors, entrepreneurs, workers and families, were wiped out by the crisis.

The nationwide destruction of prosperity was made possible by a decades-long pursuit of social justice.

The inevitability of conflict

When government grows in order to implement social justice, it also redefines the purpose of the social fabric. It is no longer there as a help to individuals in their actions and interactions. It is there to reconfigure the socio-economic organization of society. By consequence, when an economic recession or other societal crisis happens, the social fabric will not serve as a safety net or adaptation device for communities trying to cope. Instead, its purpose will be to protect the ideological values according to which the fabric has been reshaped.

In the absence of a welfare state; in other words, in the absence of a government pursuing social justice; individuals exercising responsible citizenship protect and perpetuate individual and economic freedom. Under a welfare state, the protection of freedom is replaced with the pursuit of economic redistribution. In order to achieve the desired redistribution of income, consumption and wealth, the welfare state creates a tax system and a system of entitlement programs that in combination reshape society in an egalitarian direction.

As per Rawls's theory, liberty is redefined into social justice, which in turn becomes the new purpose of government. The living conditions of every individual citizen becomes a matter of "collective social action"; a man's freedom is measured by his relative standard of living—or, in Gill's terms, the gap between his preferred choices in life and his income.

A gap between what a person wants and what he can afford becomes a matter of conflict between individuals when government decides that the person wanting more is entitled to what he cannot afford. A government that assigns entitlements will reshape the social fabric in accordance with the theory behind those entitlements. Over time, as a welfare state grows, all relationships, institutions, habits and cultural norms in a society are redefined in the image of social justice. Conflicts between unsatisfied desire and private pursuit of prosperity are built in to the welfare state's new social fabric.

Rawls stops a hair short of explicitly stating that his conflict is ingrained into an egalitarian society. Others go a little bit farther, pointing squarely to the conflict as the centerpiece of the new social fabric. For example, Karen Johnson, former University of Texas political science professor, explains that it is the state's duty to solve conflicts between "legitimate claims":[1]

> [Nozick's] assertion of each individual's absolute right to do as he pleases, so long as he does not encroach upon another's "moral space," eliminates the state as a public arena for the resolution of conflicting but legitimate claims.

The norm for solving these conflicts is Rawls's egalitarian theory of economic redistribution. So long as economic resources are abundantly available, the welfare state (which is responsible for said conflict resolution) will operate without doing any short-term structural harm to society. Its instruments for redistribution—high, progressive taxes and an elaborate system of entitlements—will not do any major, immediate harm to the economy.

However, over time the welfare state weighs down on the economy, causing "legitimate claims" to outpace available resources. This results in a slow but proliferating macroeconomic slowdown, one that is visible throughout the Western world.[2] As the "claims" conflicts gradually escalate, the social fabric is put to test. Its built-in ideological profile reveals itself in how the fabric favors economic redistribution over liberty. As the resources available for redistribution become increasingly scarce, government responds by trying to fit the ideological goal of social justice into an

---

1. See Johnson (1976, 178).
2. See Larson (2014).

increasingly tight economy. The result is an increasingly burdensome government with increasingly starved entitlement programs.[3]

In both ends, the social fabric is stressed. People's ability to cope with slowly tightening finances is paired with growing moral stress as government—having promised to cater to the many needs of the many—is gradually more austere in its delivery. Longer waiting lists for health care leave people suffering when they were promised otherwise; larger classes in schools leave children more stressed when their parents were promised otherwise; cutbacks in income security programs force people to live on tighter budgets than they were led to believe they would have to expect.

Higher taxes, which over time always accompany an increasingly austere welfare state, narrow down the scope of profitable entrepreneurship. Income, even employment, becomes stagnant, forcing people to rely more heavily on entitlements from the welfare state. As penny-pinching comes to define those entitlements, life becomes increasingly stressful.

The scrooge mentality of a welfare state under slowly escalating economic stress proliferates through the social fabric, tainting private life as well as people's economic and social relations. When an economic crisis hits, the stage is already set for a destructive destabilization of society. This was demonstrated in the Greek economic crisis, where the social fabric, designed for social justice rather than liberty, aggravated the unraveling of economic and social stability.

A life ensconced in the welfare state

There are few countries that offer a better example than Sweden of how the welfare state can transform the social fabric of a society. The transformation began in the late 1930s and was complete by the end of the 1950s.[4] My own family symbolizes this process and how it reshaped private life and relationships.

My grandparents' generation, born in the years before World War I, were raised in a society with a limited government. At that time, before the egalitarian welfare state, children grew up to live by as many of the virtues of responsible citizenship as they could. In practice, this meant providing for oneself and one's family, and never be a burden to the community.

---

3. See Larson (2018a, 2018b).
4. See Larson (2018).

Their children, born around the beginning of World War II, were also raised to understand that if you do not provide, you cannot expect anything in return. However, the welfare state, which emerged and came into full gestation during their formative years, notably affected the ethical attitudes of their generation. They came to combine a strong work ethic with an equally strong sense of entitlement: if you work and pay your taxes, you have the right to ask for all that government can provide.

My generation, born in the 1960s, moved our ethical base further away from responsible citizenship. The order of priorities was flipped, giving priority to entitlements over work ethic. We inherited the welfare-state entitlement preferences from our parents' generation and understood well to demand what government promised us. At the other end of the equation, an understanding of work ethic was still present in our generational character, but its ties to entitlements were less obvious.

The shift in focus, from "first work then entitlements" to "first entitlements then work", marks the end of the transformation process that rewrites the social fabric under a welfare state. Where my parents' generation worked to both pay taxes and provide for their families, my generation reduced the issue of having a job to a matter mostly of personal satisfaction. That the welfare state necessitates a very high rate of workforce participation was not a matter of concern to us—not until the deep economic crisis of the early 1990s turned the welfare state from generous to stingy and unwilling to deliver on its promises.

No welfare state is ever designed to provide for all the needs in life, yet its ideological goal—complete egalitarianism in the form of social justice—drives its relentless expansion. There is no other end to the growth of a welfare state than that defined by Rawls: the elimination of economic differences in society. Since this expansion eventually causes economic stagnation, the tensions that cause a destructive crisis in the social fabric will inevitably arise.

Due to the transformation of the social fabric, a society with a welfare state is almost immune to any reforms that would mitigate the inevitable crisis. As in Sweden, once a generation has been raised to embrace egalitarianism, it has also learned to take tax-paid entitlements for granted. All relationships, private and public, are implicitly colored by this notion of entitlement; to propose radical, libertarian reforms to a welfare state is to turn oneself into an outcast.[5]

---

5. With my generation's children, this has changed somewhat. They were born into

Corruption of the Social Fabric

So deep is the egalitarian programming of the social fabric that it even changes language. In 1972, British journalist Roland Huntford published *The New Totalitarians*, a unique and impressively accurate study of Sweden under the world's most elaborate egalitarian welfare state.

Huntford walks his reader through almost every dimension of Swedish society, from politics through the economy to culture, even the language itself. At every turn, he explains how the welfare state has destructively transformed society and degraded the individual into an instrument for the pursuit of social justice. He sheds his chilling spotlight on how the ideology behind the welfare state has, literally, changed the social fabric: government created a comfort zone outside of which people were no longer able to live.

Huntford offers a well-chosen example of what this means (p. 168–9):

> The Swede rarely talks about social welfare or the Welfare State. The concept which obsesses him is something rather more profound. It is an extreme form of security in all its senses, expressed in an untranslatable native word, *trygghet*. It means both safety and security: the safety of a harbor in a storm, and the security of the womb. It implies the absence of all things unpleasant and uncomfortable, and always has a connotation of escape from danger or of a frightened child running to his mother. It is perhaps the most belaboured word in the Swedish political vocabulary; no orator will speak without mentioning it; all slogans must contain it.

A native Swede could not have come up with a better definition of this word. It reveals how the welfare state has been encoded into the social fabric.

A proximate translation of *trygghet* would be "ensconced"—Swedes strive to live their lives ensconced in the welfare state. This desire, brought about by an ideologically driven transformation of almost every aspect of private life, can be summarized into the word "ensconcement".

The desire for *ensconcement* has numerous consequences, across the entire range of people's lives. The most important of them is the loss of a dynamic, long-term view of society. There is an implicit yet subtly omnipresent idea that the world is somehow static. When government assumes universal responsibility for people's lives, individual citizens no longer have

---

the deep economic crisis of the 1990s, have grown up in an unforgiving economy and never known another welfare state than that which is austere and stingy. A new attitude, more favorable to new solutions, has begun to emerge as the Millennial generation begins to draw the inevitable conclusions from having to work notably harder than our generation to even establish themselves economically.

a need to take reasoned responsibility for their own lives, let alone society as whole. All that is required is a short-sighted, mostly passionate pursuit of basic pleasure; there is no longer any need for society—or for the people—to evolve.

In a society engineered to this the Swedish degree, only one challenge remains for each citizen: to find a place in the social context, inside the life template provided by the welfare state.

It goes without saying that even if government tries to convince people that they can live in static comfort under the welfare state, the clock of economic stagnation keeps ticking. Eventually, the welfare state begins crumbling under its own weight, becoming the very nemesis of its own achievements. Government gradually loses the ability to provide for a life in ensconcement.

That is the point when social and economic destruction happens.

Uncertainty

When government makes a promise to deliver on a need shared by all—health care is a good example—it also assumes the responsibility to deliver, often while eliminating people's ability to provide for that same need independently of government. Private alternatives become impossible, legally or economically, or both.

The default on that delivery is a hard experience for those relying on government. A default on a universal promise has universal consequences; since government institutions embed themselves in the social fabric, and since the social fabric serves as a support function for confidence and forward-looking individual plans, a universal default creates ripple effects throughout society and the economy.

So far, no welfare state in the Western world has defaulted universally. However, as explained in Larson (2014), the crises in Greece, Spain, Portugal, Italy and—to a lesser degree—other European countries during the Great Recession of 2008, were exemplary case studies of government partially defaulting on its entitlement promises.

Putting aside the economic consequences of such defaults, there is a moral case to be made against the welfare state, based on these default experiences. There is a conventional wisdom embedded in the arguments for a welfare state—and for its expansion here in the United States—that government simply will not walk away from its promises. Yet even a cursory examination of the aforementioned countries during the depth of the economic crisis, shows that government is by no means immune to promise defaults.

When government assumes responsibility for our needs, its legal or economic elimination of private alternatives drastically increases the moral obligation on government shoulders. In the private sector, a business owner who loses sales can pursue new markets and make other adjustments to recover the income he has lost. A worker who is laid off can go out and apply for other jobs, if necessary even move to where opportunities are better. None of this is possible in the face of a promise default by government.

The price of a moral default by government is the uncertainty of the future that opens up in government's absence. Economist John Maynard Keynes offers a compelling example for private businesses that lends itself well to the example of government default. Illustrating the impact of uncertainty, Keynes explains what happens when people decide to reduce their consumption (for whatever reason) and put the money in the bank instead:[6]

> An act of individual saving means—so to speak—a decision not to have dinner today. But it does not necessitate a decision to have dinner or to buy a pair of boots a week hence or a year hence or to consume any specified thing at any specified date. Thus it depresses the business of preparing today's dinner without stimulating the business of making ready for some future act of consumption.

In other words, consumers spend less money today, causing businesses to lose sales today without any tangible prospect of an increase in sale in the foreseeable future. If the downturn in consumer spending is widespread throughout the economy, it causes a recession.

There is nothing remarkable in itself about this example as the starting point of a downturn in economic activity. Nor is there anything remarkable about recessions per se; a free-market economy always recovers from a recession.

The rare exceptions we know as depressions are in a category of their own, one worth examining at a later point in time. For now, the point with Keynes' example is to highlight the consequences for individual economic decisions that follow when uncertainty replaces confidence. To the business owner, what matters now is to try his best to regain sales, to attract new

---

6. See Keynes (1936, ch. 16).

customers and to make every other effort in his power to secure future revenue.

A family experiences a similar threat to their future when its breadwinner is laid off. Just as Keynes describes how a business owner has no tangible proof of future spending to rely on, a laid-off worker is hurled into uncertainty if he has no tangible new job offer to consider. In both cases, their immediate decisions will be to minimize the costs of living for the family and the costs of operation for the business. The next decision will be to pursue new revenue, i.e., an alternative way of obtaining the desired outcome of their economic activities.

Suppose, instead, that Keynes's example were about government making cuts to surgical procedures in a single-payer health care system:

> An act of cutting spending means—so to speak—a decision not to provide surgery today. But it does not necessitate a decision to provide that same surgery a week hence or a year hence or at any specified date. Thus it deprives patients of surgical procedures today without readying for the provision of those procedures at some future point in time.

Under the free market, where the entrepreneur loses sales and a family loses income, every individual is free to use his skills and talents to their fullest extent to replace what has been lost. Furthermore, in a society driven by responsible citizenship, those who fall on hard times through no fault of their own will have access to charitable help as a last resort. Thus, the opportunities and the helping hand mitigate the suffering caused by a sudden, impactful loss of earnings.

Under a government-run health care system—or any other system run by government—the individual citizen has no alternative to pursue. The welfare state replaces his confidence in the future delivery of health care with genuine uncertainty.

While uncertainty in general is a fact of life, we are equipped with the ability to handle it, under liberty, through voluntary interaction with others. That ability is expressed in our desire to try to predict the future in all its aspects, to make the future imaginable and compatible with our own ambitions.[7] To deprive a man of that ability; to thwart his desire to make the future predictable; is to deprive him of a vital part of his economic freedom.

---

7. See Schackle (1992).

It is this very deprivation that results from a broken government promise. In an isolated instance, such as a budget cut in a limited part of a single-payer health care system, the impact on individuals is serious in that part, but it does not have systemically destabilizing consequences for society as a whole. However, when a welfare state over time is subject to gradually increased fiscal stress (due, again, to a long-term slowdown in economic growth) the need for budget cuts spreads across all sections of the welfare state. As a result, the impact of the slowly rising stress on government's promises, will spread evenly as well as comprehensively across society and the economy.

Once low-intensity fiscal stress erupts into a major economic crisis, drastic spending cuts will hit all sectors of the welfare state. Government monopolies on education, health care, income security and other areas of private life deprive people of venues to mitigate uncertainty. Therefore, mounting uncertainty will rapidly spread through the social fabric, with considerable and destructive impact on society and the economy.

The moral fallacy of the closed system

In a classic paper from 1950, economist Armen Alchian explains the role that knowledge plays in building confidence in our own ability to foresee the future—and to benefit from correct foresight. On the one hand, we built knowledge based on the idea that we can get enough information of perfectly foresee the future; on the other hand, we build knowledge fully aware that the world is "open," and we can never have perfect foresight.[8]

Intuitively, it is difficult to accept that there is any meaning to any conversation about the closed system where people can have perfect foresight. After all, nobody can ever perfectly predict the future.

Yet under the welfare state, government operates as if it has perfect foresight. When it offers its services and benefits, while legally or economically eliminating all alternatives, it acts as though it can foresee all future circumstances that could affect its delivery of said services and benefits. When the welfare state creates its entitlement systems, monopolizing the needs that it provides for, it assumes that its ability to provide what it has promised will never fail.

A free-market economy, by contrast, is set up to allow people to adapt and adjust to unforeseen circumstances by innovating and trying bold, new

8. See Alchian (1950).

solutions to unsolved problems. In times of uncertainty, there is a particularly great need for entrepreneurs and investors willing to make a leap of faith. Some will hesitate, knowing that "in times of uncertainty, he who hesitates is saved to make a decision another day". Others will risk it all, fail or strike it rich.

The freedom to control one's own future is an indispensable part of what it means to be human. The freedom to form families, bonds of trust and relationships of business and charity, on a voluntary basis, is quintessential to the fomenting of strong, resilient communities. Such communities, in turn, provide the best possible environment in which to endure times of uncertainty. When personal and professional relationships are based on voluntary participation, they are also based on the presumption of mutual gain.

The freedom in participation means the freedom to change the circumstances of those relations, in other words to control and change the content of those relations. The pursuit of mutual gain means that new solutions to unsolved problems are met with the best possible scrutiny: when others willing to risk their money and their time by buying a new product or taking a job for a new business, it is a validation of a bold entrepreneurial idea. When they refrain—when they choose to make a decision another day—the entrepreneur is told to come back with a different idea.

In a society under liberty, the totality of voluntary interaction and the pursuit of mutual gain makes the community resilient in the face of hard times and unforeseen challenges. It is, in essence, the product of humans at the height of their potential. However, its accomplishments in this regard are due entirely to the fact that a society that ranks the individual as superior to the state, also recognizes that the world is "open" and perfect foresight is impossible.

Every man is endowed by his Creator with the inalienable right to life, liberty and in the pursuit of happiness. When the welfare state imposes its closed system on an open world, it morally violates the very liberty of all men subjected to its entitlement programs.

This point is counter-intuitive to many who consider a tax-paid entitlement an expansion of liberty. However, to do so is to think of liberty in the commodified sense of social-justice theory. Under American liberty, a man's freedom does not expand because he is given work-free money, goods and services; a man's freedom is expanded because government refrains from trying to alter the outcomes of his actions and interactions.

Corruption of the Social Fabric

That government is a moral government—and a government that leaves the social fabric to free, independent individuals to form and evolve.

6

Challenging American Liberty

Property Rights

THE WELFARE STATE DOES violence to both the social fabric of society and to liberty:

- It corrupts the social fabric by imposing forced solutions to human problems and needs; inevitably, the imposition of its closed-system institutions fractures the social fabric and sends society into economic degeneration;
- It restricts liberty by depriving people of choices and the freedom to innovate their way out of a crisis.

Given the incompatibility of the welfare state with human nature, it is valid to ask what drives its proponents in the first place. Theoretically, the desire to improve upon people's lives is entirely respectable; social justice advocates are generally as well-intended as their opponents. However, in practice the answer is less obvious. Again, the Bible points in the right direction (1 Sam. 8:1–3):

> And it came to pass, when Samuel was old, that he made his sons judges over Israel. Now, the name of his firstborn was Joel; and the name of his second, Abia: they were judges in Beersheba. And his sons walked not in his ways, but turned aside after lucre, and took bribes, and perverted judgment.

In other words, the judges took a personal interest in conflict arbitration. Passion rose above reason; the power that came with their position corrupted them morally. In the same fashion, the modern state invites moral corruption, for those who hold elected offices as well as those who have—or can obtain—the power to regulate private life.

Beyond the minimal state, the turn after lucre can manifest itself in the creation of new government programs, entitlements, proposed again by well-intended egalitarians as a means to help those who live in tough circumstances. However, to a politician or a government administrator, such programs become tools of power and, even more importantly, a badge of accomplishment.

At the end of a work day, business owners can list the goods or services they have sold to their customers and go to bed with a sense of accomplishment. An engineer can point to the bridge he designed and helped build; a teacher can take pride in what his students have learned; a physician has the patients he has cured.

A legislator has no such measurements of accomplishment. His production consists exclusively of the bills he voted for—and the money he appropriated. A government administrator has the department he manages, measured by the appropriations he receives from the legislature. He also has the benefits he pays out to people through entitlement programs. The more spending he approves; the more employees he has working under him; the greater the sense of accomplishment in government administration.

None of this is new. God explained to the Israelites precisely what would happen when judges were elevated to kings:[1]

- Government will build its own workforce;
- Taxes will pay for this workforce;
- It will be used to select groups that will be deemed entitled to government handouts; and
- Government will provide for the people what the people otherwise would provide for themselves.

This is the modern form of lucre that morally corrupts government. But the corruption goes deeper. When government imposes its moral values on society; when its pursuit of economic redistribution rewrites the social fabric; those who are in a position to select the entitled population

---

1. 1. Sam. 8:5, 8:11–17, 8:20.

are in a position to select and de-select individuals. Under a government health-care monopoly, some patients will be given care, while others will not.

The power to make these choices is another, modern form of lucre. It is present in American society today, making itself known as an ideological shift in the purpose of government institutions. In Europe, where this transformation took place earlier and, in many countries, faster than in America, the process appears to have reached the point of no return—it is irreversible. Without a radical remake of the entire socio-economic structure; without a return to an open-system social fabric; most European countries have no path back to classical liberalism (the closest European counterpart to American liberty).

Here in the United States, the transformation process has not been as fast and not as decisive. It is close to irreversible, though: essentially, the continuation of "business as usual" in terms of welfare state growth will soon bring American culture, its society and the economy past the point where the only future is one of economically and morally repressive social justice.

Parliamentary democracy vs. the constitutional republic

The pursuit of social justice can even shape our form of government. Parliamentary democracy is a conduit for social justice, while a constitutional republic of the American kind hampers its progress. There is no social-justice purpose in parliamentary democracy—in fact, the term "democracy" has rightfully gained prominent status in the modern, Western world. However, its mode of operation has proven to benefit rapid, government-imposed societal change, while the constitutional republic is designed to favor inertia.

Originally, "demos kratia" referred to direct popular government in ancient Greece; today, with the volume of legislation needed in a modern welfare state, direct popular rule is impossible. To manage the complex system that is the welfare state, we have created a new profession: the legislator. However, it is not the legislative profession in itself that drives the growth in government; it is a facilitating factor as legislators build resumes with accomplishments like all professionals. The key to government growth is instead the egalitarian ideology of social justice, the advancement of which is facilitated by the legislative structure of parliamentary democracy.

The core of parliamentary democracy is the idea that a majority vote is the final word on legislation. This is the case especially in the regular legislative process, but it also applies to elections. A majority vote, first in an election and then in parliament, is presumed to be sufficient as due legislative process; the outcomes are considered just precisely because they were the result of majority vote.

In a constitutional republic, electoral and legislative majority votes are restricted by two measures, put in place to protect individual liberty. The first measure is the division of government branches: where a parliamentary system bundles together the executive and legislative branches of government—in some cases even the judicial branch—a constitutional republic separates them. Voters have to cast their ballots in separate elections depending on branch of government; if they see undue expansion of government in one branch, they can balance it up by voting for more restrictions from the other branch.

No such balance of powers exists in a parliamentary democracy. The common procedure is that the legislative majority appoints a prime minister, whose job is to run the executive branch. This makes it easier for a popular majority to affect change and reform as they see fit; it also reduces the ability of the people to take corrective measures if they see a runaway political agenda.

The other restrictive measure in a constitutional republic is the Constitution itself. Even if a majority of voters elect a Congress that wants to abolish the First Amendment, reinstitute slavery or confiscate all private property, the Constitution makes it practically impossible for Congress to do so, especially in the expedient manner it can be done in a parliamentary democracy. Furthermore, it is exceedingly difficult to change the U.S. Constitution; e.g., it requires votes by 99 legislative chambers, with an affirmative majority in three quarters of them (38 states) and both chambers of U.S. Congress. However, even before a controversial piece of legislation begins its path through that arduous process, the Constitution gives the third branch of government, the judiciary, the same independent status as the executive and legislative branches. One feature of this independence is that the Supreme Court is the final arbiter of the Constitution.

An illustration of the difference between parliamentary democracy and the constitutional republic can run through many different examples. However, in the modern world there are few that stand out with such chilling clarity as the expropriation of private property. Not only does the taking of property affect a core institution of the free market—property rights—but it also serves as an arena for the ideological conflict between egalitarianism and libertarianism. The former, we remember, ranks the state above the individual, demoting the individual to instrumental status in government policy; the latter ranks the individual above the state, confining the latter to limited, enumerated functions in support of private life.

The reasons for property expropriation are directly or indirectly dependent on the ideological motive behind the expropriation. It is not the taking of land per se that constitutes the ideological act—the U.S. Constitution allows for eminent-domain seizure of private property—but the motive for the taking. The following sections discuss different examples, and how different motives interact with the form of government within which they take place.

The dangers with parliamentary democracy

When the majority is right by default, it is right regardless of the end result of its decisions. This means that the majority is entrusted with the responsibility to always make the "right" decision. In lieu of any ideological motive behind majority parliamentary votes, it is an open question what that really means. It could be that the majority always rules with the utmost protection of individual freedom in mind, but there are only weak safeguards in place against a legislative majority that promotes its own interest at the explicit expense of the minority.

In theory, a parliamentary system allows for a majority to institute slavery, impose dictatorship or pass any number of equally atrocious bills. Unlike the U.S. system, where two legislative chambers—and an elected individual—have to approve a bill before it becomes law, parliamentary democracy relies entirely on one majority vote.

In practice, there are constitutional hurdles in the way of legislation that is too radical. However, even here, the procedure is often designed to protect and facilitate majority rule under all circumstances. Overall, the parliamentary system puts individual liberty in jeopardy by virtue of its unmitigated reliance on majority rule.

South Africa is a compelling example of what this means in practice. The country's parliament has an ideological agenda for economic redistribution that includes expropriation of land. As of January 2019, this agenda is expected to be within months of implementation. Specifically, the goal is to take land from white farmers and giving it to blacks.

The idea of land expropriation is not new. It has been around ever since the African National Congress (ANC) took over government at the end of Apartheid in 1994. Over the years the motive for expropriation has gradually shifted, from restitution of historic injustices—returning land in instances where it was illegally taken from black farmers—to economic redistribution. The restitution argument can still be heard in the public debate, but it has never been shown how large a share of white farmers sit on land that was gotten through theft.

There is a major difference between expropriation for restitutional purposes and for social-justice reasons. If it is a matter of restitution, the return of property to the rightful owners (in person or their posterity) is a legitimate process to uphold the institution of the property right. This would be a matter of defending the freedom of the original owners and therefore make expropriation a legitimate function of a minimal state. If, on the other hand, the purpose is social justice, thus turning land expropriation into a means for economic redistribution, it will violate—as opposed to protect—individual freedom.

It is in this context that the parliamentary system of South Africa becomes relevant. The country has a bicameral parliament, with one chamber—the National Assembly—being elected through universal suffrage. The other, called the National Council of Provinces, is appointed by the provincial governments. In terms of regular legislation, majority votes in both chambers are sufficient to pass a bill into law. However, it is not that much more difficult to change the South African constitution, a fact that has become pertinent in the debate over land expropriation. On August 24, 2018, the Daily Maverick, a South African news outlet, reported:[2]

> South Africa's most strident political supporter of expropriation without compensation, EFF President Julius Malema, has warned the ANC government against its plans to begin expropriating land immediately and accused President Cyril Ramaphosa of misleading voters on his commitment to land reform. Malema ... called for the Constitution to be amended before land is expropriated. ... "If you expropriate before [amending the Constitution] you risk a court battle with all those who own properties you seek to expropriate," said Malema.

2. See: https://www.dailymaverick.co.za/article/2018-08-24-dont-expropriate-land-until-constitution-is-amended-julius-malema/

From an American viewpoint, this sounds like a prudent approach to a contested issue. However, unlike its American counterpart the South African constitution is not a rigid document. It is easy for parliament to alter it, the main rule being that the constitution can be changed by means of one vote in parliament with a two-thirds majority in both chambers (there are slight variations depending on what part of the constitution is targeted).

In other words, the procedure for changing the South African constitution is approximately similar to if the United States Senate and House could vote, each one of them once, and with a 2/3 majority add, repeal or rewrite sections in the Constitution.

To a radical politician in America, who wants to drastically change the country, our current procedure for Constitutional amendments is an almost insurmountable obstacle. By contrast, a South African politician who wants radical policies implemented can patiently wait for a re-write of pertinent sections of his country's founding document. But that is not all: in addition to making constitutional reforms with relative ease, Mr. Malema and other South African radicals can morally justify their policies by pointing to the constitution. So long as the South African parliament makes the appropriate change to the constitution, land expropriation without compensation becomes morally validated.

The reason for this is the reliance on the majority vote: when the majority is always right, its decisions are always moral. The majority vote is in fact the jurisdiction that defines morality; it is worth noting that the South African constitution has no anchor for individual rights. Unlike the United States, the South African nation does not constitutionally protect individual rights against majority-rule abuse.

Herein lies a philosophical presumption: the individual is subordinate to the majority; a majority vote defines the boundaries of what is right and wrong. Legislation is always justified by the majority rule.

Bluntly, the state is superior to the individual.

To reiterate: if the expropriation of land were only about restituting an injustice committed under Apartheid, there would be no problem with government seizing one man's land to give it to its rightful original proprietor. In fact, this restitutional expropriation function should have been made explicit in the first post-Apartheid constitution of 1994; it was not. That aside, a change to make it constitutional is legitimate by libertarian principles. In fact, it would be incumbent upon the South African government to return land to those, from whom it has been stolen—or their rightful heirs—and to do so without delay.

However, as the African National Congress (ANC) has made clear, expropriation is primarily, if not exclusively, about economic redistribution.[3] Because of its exclusive reliance on majority votes for legislation, the parliamentary system easily becomes a conduit for all kinds of ideologies. There are no value biases in the system itself, a fact that is apparent in the South African case, especially its constitution. It makes no distinction between between land expropriation for restitution and for redistribution; what has kept the South African government from widespread redistributive land expropriation is its desire to redistribute without compensating those, from whom land is taken.

Economic redistribution is more effective when there is no compensation given to those who are forced to surrender property. A taxpayer giving up part of his income or wealth to fund a welfare state, is not granted partial compensation for the taxes he pays.

In a form of government where there are no checks and balances on majority rule; where, bluntly, the majority is assumed to always be right; there is no moral difference between one man's property rights and another man's social-justice issued entitlement. It is up to the majority to rank one of them higher than the other. If priority is given to the property right, the majority conveys a libertarian ideology in its legislation; if priority is given to entitlements, the majority adopts egalitarian social justice.

In parliamentary democracy, the legislative method is a conveyor belt for the majority and its ideology of choice. The legislative means justify the ideological ends.

By consequence, the parliamentary system allows ideological currents in public opinion to make rapid, radical changes to a country. The assumption of moral validity in unmitigated majority rule is widely shared, expressing itself in prominent support for the South African government's land expropriation plans. For example, on August 30, 2018, Reuters reported that the International Monetary Fund has given its blessing to land expropriation for the purposes of economic redistribution, provided the process is constitutional. The IMF even explicitly gave its blessing to land expropriation strictly for the purpose of economic redistribution, i.e., social justice:[4]

---

3. See: http://www.anc.org.za

4. See: https://www.reuters.com/article/us-safrica-imf/imf-supports-south-african-land-reform-provided-its-rules-based-idUSKCN1LF1FX

> The International Monetary Fund gave its full backing to South Africa's land reform plan on Thursday, as long as the highly contentious process is transparent and based on the constitution. The Fund's senior resident representative in South Africa Montfort Mlachila told Reuters that … "We are in full support of the need to undertake land reforms in order to address the issues of inequality," Mlachila said in an interview.

British prime minister Theresa May agrees. On August 28, 2018, Independent Online quoted Mrs. May as saying:[5]

> The UK has for some time now supported land reform. Land reform that is legal, that is transparent, that is generated through a democratic process. It's an issue that I raised and discussed with President Ramaphosa when he was in London earlier this year. I'll be talking about it with him later today.

With these words, the British prime minister is in full agreement with Julius Malema, the leader of the radical Economic Freedom Fighters. So long as the South African parliament changes the constitution to legalize land expropriation for the sole purpose of economic redistribution, even without compensation, the taking of land is morally acceptable.[6]

It does not matter that the South African constitution formally protects private property.[7] This token gesture is no match for the national parliament, which has full jurisdiction over the constitution. In short, since all it takes is a two-thirds majority vote in each of the two chambers of the parliament, constitutionally guaranteed individual rights are only moderately more protected than rights established by statute.[8]

Some parliamentary democracies have a somewhat more rigid procedure for changing the constitution. In Denmark, the parliament can vote with a simple majority in favor of a constitutional change, but it does not have full jurisdiction over the process. A general election must be held and

---

5. See: https://www.iol.co.za/news/politics/britain-supports-land-reform-in-sa-pm-theresa-may-16775862

6. The Independent Online also gave voice to an opposing view: *Gerard Batten, leader of UKIP, slammed May's comments saying: "Theresa May says she supports land reform in South Africa that is legal. Many countries in the world have taken actions which are 'legal', but that doesn't make them morally right."*

7. Chapter 2, Section 25, Clause 2: https://dearsouthafrica.co.za/wp-content/uploads/2018/05/SAConstitution-web-eng.pdf

8. See: https://www.gov.za/documents/constitution/Constitution-Republic-South-Africa-1996-1

the newly elected parliament must approve the exact same bill with a simple majority. After that, a referendum must be held, where at least 40 percent of the voting-age population vote in favor.[9]

The Danish amendment procedure is a typical compromise under a unitary state with centralized legislative powers. The ability of the parliament to govern the country as it sees fit is weighed against "reasonable" measures to prevent runaway legislation. However, the very fact that it is a compromise shows the problem when the first duty of government is majority rule rather than protection of individual liberty.

The Swedish parliamentary system is closer to the South African in terms of constitutional rigidity—or lack thereof. As in Denmark, the Swedish constitution requires two simple-majority parliamentary votes, with an election in between, but the parliament retains full jurisdiction over the constitutional change. Unlike Denmark, Sweden does not require a referendum.

By comparison, the process for amending the U.S. constitution (the only way to make changes to it) is formidably complicated, requiring

a) A two-thirds vote in favor, not by one, but by two legislative chambers, namely both the House of Representatives and the United States Senate; and

b) The ratification by three quarters of the 50 states.

Unlike parliamentary systems with only one legislative body, whether single-chamber (Denmark, Sweden) or bicameral (South Africa), the U.S. procedure is far more rigid. It involves 50 legislative bodies with 99 legislative chambers.[10] This means that including Congressional approval, a constitutional amendment must pass in 76 different legislative chambers.

The process is rigid, not to say arduous, explaining why the U.S. Constitution is so rarely amended. With the exception of the Bill of Rights, it has only happened 17 times in almost 250 years. There is a reason for this high threshold: it is there to give the constitution the rigidity needed to

---

9. The 40-percent number may seem odd, given that it is not a majority of the voting population. It serves as a compromise between the need to avoid approval by a small number of voters (if, for example, a large number of voters refused or were coerced into not participating) and the need to allow an amendment vote to proceed even under adverse conditions.

10. Every state has a house of representatives and a senate, except Nebraska which is unicameral.

protect individual citizens from undue infringements on their rights by their own government—or the majority of their fellow citizens.

This last point is fundamentally important. The ideology of American liberty prescribes that every single citizen be protected against transgressions by the majority. For clarity, this does not mean that majority votes are inherently immoral or infringe liberty; majority votes are inherently void of morality. It is the purpose behind the vote that grants its moral status.

From a practical viewpoint, it is not possible for a state to exist without a venue for majority votes to move legislation forward. However, for precisely this reason, the constitutional protection of individual liberty must serve as a condition for majority rule.

In addition to the rigidity of the amendment process, the separation of powers in the U.S. Constitution gives both the executive and judicial branches ability to stop runaway majority rule. In addition to the separation of the three branches of government, as in the constitutional amendment process, there is also a vertical separation between federal and state powers. No parliamentary system exhibits the same adherence to checks, balances and accountability. Therefore, no parliamentary system is as inherently prone to preservation of values built into the founding document as the American constitutional republic.

American liberty jeopardized: Kelo v. New London

The U.S. Constitution is designed to further libertarianism which, in combination with Christian ethics, forms the ideology of American liberty. Its foremost character trait is to elevate the individual above the state, confining the state to a set of enumerated functions. Furthermore, the Constitution is designed to discourage reforms that weaken its protection of American liberty. This, however, does not mean that its form of government is immune to egalitarian advances. A strong testimony to this is in the emergence and expansion of an egalitarian welfare state during the latter half of the 20th century.

When writing the Constitution, the Founding Fathers did not pretend to create an insurmountable bulwark against changes to the ideology they had penned into it. All they could provide were the tools of government that would best help future generations to preserve, protect and expand on American liberty. In fact, its foremost protection is in the daily business of government as well as private lives. When the practice of American liberty is lost, its protection in the Constitution begins to wither.

There are few examples of this as blatant as the legal case of *Kelo v. City of New London*. It resembles the South African case of land expropriation, though its immediate consequences are of course far less serious. It illustrates how values of social justice can change the practice of government in the United States, without changing the written word of the Constitution.

Specifically, *Kelo* resembles the South African case in how:

- Egalitarian thought turns the relationship between the individual and the state upside down, compared to how it is defined in American liberty; and
- Doing so can upset one of the most important components of economic and individual freedom, namely the property right.

Susette Kelo was a property owner in the Fort Trumbull neighborhood of New London, a city in Connecticut. As part of an economic development project, the city wanted to seize Ms. Kelo's home as well as numerous other properties. The city planned to replace them with new private property that would bring more tax revenue to the city. Ms. Kelo sued the city and the case eventually made its way up to the U.S. Supreme Court, where it was heard and decided in 2005.

The *Kelo* case was the culmination of a multi-year effort by the city of New London to grow its tax base. A key point of this plan was the recruitment of Pfizer, the pharmaceutical company, to build a research facility in New London. Explains the Institute for Justice:[11]

> In 1998, pharmaceutical giant Pfizer built a plant next to Fort Trumbull and the City determined that someone else could make better use of the land than the Fort Trumbull residents. The City handed over its power of eminent domain—the ability to take private property for public use—to the New London Development Corporation (NLDC), a private body, to take the entire neighborhood for private development.

It is important to note that the explicit purpose behind the eminent domain case against Ms. Kelo et al was to collect more taxes from properties in the Fort Trumbull area. That revenue, in turn, would replenish the city's General Fund, thus paying for both constitutional government

---

11. See: https://ij.org/case/kelo/

functions—the protection of life, liberty and property, - and redistributive functions such as welfare, health care, education or so-called economic development. Therefore, the purpose of economic redistribiton is not as explicit as in the South Africa case. However, the case also elevates egalitarianism in its demotion of the individual relative the state; conditions are placed on property rights, subordinating those rights to the needs of government.

In fact, herein lies the *Kelo* case's most prominent advancement of egalitarian social justice. The City of New London wanted to take the properties in Fort Trumbull in order to increase its tax revenue, but it never specified what functions that new tax revenue would pay for. This left it open for the city to use it squarely for economic redistribution, i.e., the advancement of social justice. More importantly, though: since the case went all the way up to the Supreme Court and was judged in favor of the city, the city's open-ended use of the tax revenue was now granted constitutional status.

In theory, every state, county, city and township in the country could now take private property as part of a pursuit of more tax revenue—exclusively for the purposes of redistributing income and wealth. If a property owner is not providing the welfare state with enough tax revenue, he could face eminent domain.

Subordinating property rights to social justice

The *Kelo* case breaks down into two parts, both of which demonstrate the advancement of egalitarian thinking within the realm of the U.S. Constitution. The first part was the question of whether more tax revenue was a legitimate cause for eminent domain. The second part was the question whether or not a private entity could pursue eminent domain against another private entity. The city farmed out its eminent domain case against Ms. Kelo et al to the New London Development Corporation, NLDC, a so-called economic development corporation.

By making property rights conditional upon their contribution to the tax base, the NLDC came to pursue an eminent-domain case charged with ideological conflict. Under American liberty, so long as a property is rightfully acquired through original work (I worked with my own hands and built a chair) or through voluntary exchange (the chair was purchased, inherited or given as a gift), the property right cannot be terminated. The only exception is a narrow window of public use. The ideological conflict was concentrated to this term.

The conflict pinned American liberty against social justice: where American liberty does not permit the taking of property for anything except the narrowest definition of public use—infrastructure or other constitutional functions of government—social justice subordinates property rights to the ideological pursuit of economic redistribution. In the former case, a property owner can only expect to lose his property under very limited conditions; in the latter case, he can expect to keep it so long as his property generates adequate tax revenue.

In *Kelo*, government—the city of New London—deemed that the properties in Fort Trumbull did not generate enough tax revenue. Without the case itself referring to social justice as an ideological motivating factor, the city of New London nevertheless applied its property-rights condition: it explicitly stated that it expected more tax revenue from a revocation of existing property rights.

If government believes that there is more tax revenue to be gained by means of transferring property from one owner to another, then under the ideology of social justice it has the right—even the moral obligation—to transfer property ownership. In other words, under social justice, eminent domain is reduced to a practical question. Since the goal of egalitarian public policy is to reduce economic differences between private citizens (based on Rawls's principle of maximizing the standard of living of the worst off in society) what remains of a property right is the technical issue of how to measure progress toward that goal.

By contrast, under the minimal state that is compliant with American liberty, eminent domain can only be used for public projects of two kinds: providing infrastructure and protecting life, liberty and property. Both kinds of projects are constitutional government services; when either of them requires the acquisition of private property, government—but only government—can use eminent domain.

The *Kelo* case did not confine the use of the new tax revenue to either protective functions or to expansion of infrastructure. While the city of New London did not explicitly omit specificities regarding how it would spend the new tax revenue, the absence of designated spending plans is in itself an ideological flag. Eminent domain is now linked to spending for egalitarian, social-justice purposes.

As yet another conditioning of property rights for the advancement of social justice, *Kelo* gives government full jurisdiction over the decision whether or not a property right yields enough tax revenue. The individual taxpayer is given no opportunity to object to the government's assessment of its own need for more revenue. Since the government's pursuit of more revenue takes place under a given budget, it also means that it seeks more revenue without questioning whether or not its own spending plans are excessive relative the existing tax base. Eminent domain thus becomes an instrument for expanding the tax base so that government does not have to make reductions—temporary or structural—in its budget.

A large part of the budgets in modern governments, state as well as local, is devoted to economic redistribution. An estimate from available statistical sources suggests that states and local governments use at least half of their budgets to comply with egalitarian ideological goals.[12] Since the programs fulfilling those goals were not questioned before the *Kelo* eminent-domain case was opened, it is at least implicit in the actions of the city government that social-justice policies are a perfectly legitimate reason to revoke property rights.

A property owner's rights are subordinated to an explicit ideological agenda, with the ideology of social justice de facto being made a reason for eminent domain.

To further demote property rights, *Kelo* opened for private parties to pursue eminent domain against private property owners on the grounds of improving tax revenue. It was, namely, not the city of New London that pursued eminent domain. The party in question, the NLDC, was a private 501(c)(3) non-profit entity.

It is important to take a minute and understand this part of the *Kelo* case. The NLDC, a private entity, was never asked to verify its claim that it could increase the city's tax revenue.

Since its founding in 1978, the NLDC had spelled out its purpose as preventing blight and helping businesses invest and develop in the city of New London. Throughout its life it has maintained this status; as of 2018, under its new name, Renaissance City Development Association (RCDA), it presents itself as[13]

---

12. See the Census Bureau, State Government Finance database, for raw data. For a less precise but comparable database, see the National Association of State Budget Officers, Annual State Expenditure Reports.

13. See: http://www.rcda.co/what-we-do-new-london-ct/

a not-for-profit community development corporation comprised of citizens, business owners and community leaders of New London, Connecticut.

In other words, a private entity.

Notably, when the Supreme Court wrote its syllabus in the *Kelo* case it explained (emphasis added):[14]

> After approving an integrated development plan designed to revitalize its ailing economy, respondent city, *through its development agent*, purchased most of the property earmarked for the project from willing sellers

In other words, the Supreme Court did not find it relevant that the NLDC actually was a private entity. Therefore, it also ignored the fact that a private entity was suing another private entity under eminent domain for the sole purpose of increasing tax revenue for a third party—the city government.

Justice O'Connor, however, put her spotlight on this very fact. In her dissenting opinion she noted that the NDLC "is not elected by popular vote, and its directors and employees are privately appointed." Therefore, it is not a government entity, making the case one between two private parties.

By assuming that the NLDC was a government entity, the Supreme Court majority actually, and probably unintentionally, highlighted the ideological under-current of the case. By skipping over the legal-status issue of the NLDC, the Court focused the case on the government activity that led to it, namely economic development. The only tangible goal with economic development was to increase tax revenue. (That is, in fact, the prevailing purpose behind economic development in general.) In doing so, the Court majority effectively created a situation where private citizens can seek to use eminent domain against other private citizens. All they need to do is suggest that the eminent-domain action will likely increase tax revenue for government.

By making a desire to increase tax revenue a sufficient reason for eminent domain, and by allowing a private entity to pursue that revenue increase, the Supreme Court established egalitarianism as a predominant ideology in eminent-domain cases. To see the practical meaning in this, consider the following example.

---

14. *Kelo et al v. City of New London et al*, 545 U.S. 469 (2005).

A wealthy man is looking for a new home. He sees a property in a desirable location and offers to buy it. The property owner turns down his generous offer. The wealthy man could take the property owner to court, claiming that he will build a substantially more luxurious property that will yield much more in property taxes. Furthermore, he could make the case that his income is so much higher than the current owners that his income taxes will make a notable difference to the city's bottom line.

Alternatively, he could convince a local economic-development entity to pursue eminent domain on his behalf.

Is this an inconceivable scenario? Suppose the very wealthy man is a property developer who promises to replace existing, fully functional, non-blighted homes with a billionaire's row of upscale condominiums.

When social-justice motivated pursuit of more tax revenue is a legitimate cause for eminent domain, the point of protection for private property has been moved. The question left open by the *Kelo* case is: where along the line from a major property developer to the wealthy individual going after one house is a property owner protected against eminent domain?

Public purpose: egalitarianism in the Fifth Amendment

In America's founding, property rights and the right to keep all income were virtually sacrosanct. In its Guide to The Constitution, the Heritage Foundation explains the reason why the Constitution does not absolutely and explicitly protect property rights. [15] The Founding Fathers took them for granted; the Takings Clause does not provide a stronger protection because

> As a matter of original understanding, the American Founders viewed the natural right to acquire or possess property as embedded in the common law, which they regarded as the natural law applied to specific facts. Thus, the Framers thought that there was little need to create a 'parchment protection' against the states, which were, after all, carrying on the common-law tradition.

The Guide also explains that James Madison, who drafted the clause, "apparently believed that the federal government, which, of course, had no long-standing tradition of supporting property rights, should be explicitly

---

15. See: https://www.heritage.org/constitution/#!/amendments/5/essays/151/takings-clause

restricted to follow the common-law form." The states already had an established tradition, imported from England, of protecting property.

In 1896, the Supreme Court confirmed this meaning of the Takings Clause. In line with the principles of American liberty, the Court established that the taking of private property for the use of another private citizen is unconstitutional.[16] In 1923, in *Cincinnati v. Vester*, the Court required of government a definitive specification of what function of government—"what public use"—the property confiscation would further.[17]

This approach to property rights and eminent domain is a far cry from that which is embedded as the ideological core of the *Kelo* case. That core, however, did not materialize in *Kelo*, but traces its roots back through a string of Supreme Court cases. *Kelo* marked the completion of a decades-long metamorphosis of the Takings Clause, to where the Court had replaced "public use" with "public purpose". The Court's definition of this term is reminiscent of the elasticity of a rubber band.

In its motivation for *Kelo*, the Supreme Court traces its "public purpose" definition of the Takings Clause all the way back to a case called *Fallbrook v. Bradley* from 1896. A property owner in California refused to pay a fee to a local irrigation district. To recover the unpaid fees, the district used eminent domain to seize his property. In response, the owner argued that the irrigation district was using the fees for private purposes, as the irrigation system benefited private lands. Therefore, the Takings Clause in the Fifth Amendment would not apply.

The Supreme Court disagreed: the irrigation of arid land was indeed in compliance with the term "public use".[18] In its majority opinion in *Kelo*, the court argued that the taking of private property was similar to *Fallbrook*.

The Court's comparison of *Kelo* to *Fallbrook* is weak, yet it carries relevance for understanding where the public-purpose definition of the Takings Clause comes from. The *Fallbrook* case was about a constitutional government function. An irrigation system, the funding of which was the motivation for eminent domain, is a piece of infrastructure and therefore comparable to railroads and highways.

In *Kelo*, the purpose was not to recover revenue for a designated purpose, but to increase revenue for unspecified use in general spending.

---

16. *Missouri Pacific Railroad Company v. Nebraska*, 164 U.S. 403, 417 (1896)

17. Nicholson and Mota (2005). See also *Old Dominion Land Company v. United States*, 269 U.S. 55 (1925).

18. *Fallbrook v. Bradley*, 164 U.S. 112 (1896).

Therefore, the beginning of the transformation of the Takings Clause is really more recent than the Court suggested in *Kelo*. That beginning is to be found in *Berman v. Parker* from 1954. This case is closer to *Kelo*, with a city—the District of Columbia—wanting to seize private homes as part of a "comprehensive plan"[19]

> to eliminate and prevent slum and substandard housing conditions—even though such property may later be sold or leased to other private interests subject to conditions designed to accomplish these purposes.

Superficially, the policy goal in *Berman* is different than in *Kelo*. The city of the District of Columbia did not seek to increase tax revenue, but to eliminate blight. In fact, at no point in its *Berman* opinion does the Court discuss tax revenue. However, the *Berman* case explicitly opens the Takings Clause to policy goals other than constitutional government functions. It was the D.C. city government itself that defined when a property was to be classified as in "substandard condition." Similarly, in the *Kelo* case it was up to the city of New London to define when a private property was inadequate as a taxpayer.

In both cases, a path is opened for government to pursue ideological goals by means of eminent domain: government decides the goal, applies it to private property and then deems that property to be unfit for the fulfillment of said ideological goal. The goals themselves differed:

- In *Berman*, the city of the District of Columbia decided that private property was not of acceptable living standard, itself determining that standard;
- In *Kelo*, the city of New London decided what spending it wanted and determined what tax base it needed in order to pay for that spending.

In both cases, private homes were condemned for not living up to the standards set by government.

Also, *Kelo* and *Berman* are ideologically similar. The term "public use" has been replaced with the term "public purpose" which in turn defines any eminent-domain case as legitimate under the Takings Clause, if by seizing it government can achieve an ideological goal of that government's choosing.

An even stronger example of this ideological shift is *Hawaii Housing Authority v. Midkiff* from 1984. Here, the Court overtly and specifically

---

19. *Berman v. Parker*, 348 U.S. 26 (1954). See Syllabus.

relied on egalitarian ideology and the theory of social justice. It ruled that it was perfectly fine to use eminent domain to redistribute private property for no other purpose than, as it explained in its opinion, to "reduce the perceived social and economic evils of a land oligopoly". The Court explained that in response to this oligopoly, which was

> traceable to the early high chiefs of the Hawaiian Islands, the Hawaii Legislature enacted the Land Reform Act of 1967 (Act), which created a land condemnation scheme whereby title in real property is taken from lessors and transferred to lessees in order to reduce the concentration of land ownership.

According to a procedure for establishing "just compensation", the Land Reform Act compensated property owners when their land was taken by government and then sold to lessees on those lands. However, the ideological charge in the Court's decision lies in its approval of land redistribution in order to fight "perceived social and economic evils of land oligopoly." Blatantly, the Court says that it is in compliance with the public-use term in the Takings Clause of the Fifth Amendment for government to take one private citizen's property and sell it to another private citizen, if the transaction reduces the economic difference between the two, or between private citizens in general.

With *Midkiff* the Supreme Court took a big step into the territory of social justice. The *Kelo* case did not go as far in terms of explicit reliance on this particular ideology: where *Midkiff* legitimized the use of social-justice ideology in eminent domain, *Kelo* opened for its expanded application by granting general use of tax revenue from forced replacement of private property.

Appendix: A theoretical point on the minimal state and eminent domain

There is a narrow grey zone just outside this philosophical definition of the minimal state, where eminent domain can be applied while still not transitioning government into the realm of the welfare state. That grey zone is not defined by libertarian theory, but by economics, and accounts for the production of "public goods".

Economic theory distinguishes between private and public goods, but the distinction is not related to who the producer of the good is. It is not the case that any product produced by government is a public good, nor is any private good private because it is produced by a private business.

A private good is a product where there is exclusion in consumption. A tube of tooth paste can only be consumed by one person at a time; when I buy that tooth paste tube, nobody else can buy the same tube. A gallon of gasoline can only go into one vehicle; a hamburger can only be eaten by one person; a hospital bed can only be used by one patient at a time.

The practical meaning of "exclusion in consumption" is that the producer of private goods can separate them and sell them for a distinct price. He can also prevent people from using the product by refusing to sell, for example if they are not willing to pay the price he asks. If he asks too high a price and prevents too many from buying it, he may eventually have to lower the price, but that is only another consequence of the fact that the product can only have one buyer at the same time.

So long as a producer can separate the units of his product, he can charge a price higher than zero for each unit. He also needs to do so, since he has a cost higher than zero to produce one more unit. That is not the case with public goods, the classic example of which is a street light. Two or more people can walk down a street at night and enjoy the illuminated sidewalk under one and the same street light.

The producer of the street light cannot separate the light on the basis of each consumer. It is not the case that he can sell one package of light to one person, without anyone else being able to enjoy the same light. Therefore, there is no exclusion in consumption and no basis for individual, market-based pricing.

On the flip side of the equation, it does not cost the producer of the street light anything more to provide that light to one more person. The same is true for a highway: with the exception of very crowded metropolitan areas in rush hour, highways can be used by every car traveling on them without excluding others from doing the same. It is not necessary for the highway owner to add an extra lane simply to let one more car travel on the highway (again with the exception of very crowded cities).

Since it is not possible to identify an individual marginal cost in the consumption of public goods, it is not possible to set a market-based price per unit sold. Theoretically, a private business can still provide a public good, such as a privately built, owned and operated highway, but in practice that would always result in a monopoly situation. Without the realistic possibility of a free market, a public good will always end up costing too much to motivate consumption or result in revenue that is too low to merit construction in the first place.

Technically, the composition of operating costs for a public good is dominated by fixed costs; the variable cost is negligible precisely because there is no marginal cost for producing one extra unit. Therefore, once one unit of a public good has been produced—such as a highway between two cities—the cost for a competitor to enter the market is prohibitively high.

Since a free market cannot provide public goods on the same terms as it can private goods, there is only one realistic situation that would allow the production, maintenance and development of public goods, namely that government be responsible for them. Government can then recover the cost for depreciation due to regular use of, e.g., a toll highway (or it can allow a private operator to recover costs and manage maintenance).

Eminent domain becomes relevant to public goods in the construction of new units. If government needs to build a new radar station for commercial air traffic, it may have to take privately owned property in the process. The purpose behind the use of eminent domain will then be compliant with the minimal state; the product—radar surveillance of air space—is not redistributive in nature.

Suppose that government did not want to take property for a public good, but for a food dispensary for low-income families. No matter how worthy one might think the cause to be, it is nevertheless a case of economic redistribution: a property is taken from one private citizen, then used to provide for a limited group of other citizens, deemed entitled based on government-sanctioned ideological criteria.

In the *Kelo* case, the city of New London went farther than that. They did not specify exactly what they were going to spend the extra tax revenue on. They wanted more tax revenue in general, dissatisfied as they were with the taxes paid by existing property owners. Like practically every other local government, the city of New London spends only part of their money on minimal-state services, with the rest going toward economic redistribution in one form or another. Therefore, the use of eminent domain is not compliant with the minimal state, but expands into the realm of the welfare state.

Some writers have suggested that eminent domain was used to remedy a market failure.[20] This is an incorrect observation; market failure is the effect of the cost structure and product nature of public goods. There was a

---

20. See: https://sites.duke.edu/djepapers/files/2016/10/Hansen.pdf

market for the properties in the Fort Trumbull area—anyone who wanted to buy those properties could make an offer to the owners. They chose not to sell, but that decision does not constitute market failure. Furthermore, even when market failure is at hand, it is not the case that government should always intervene.[21]

---

21. Feldman et al (2014). https://www.eda.gov/files/tools/research-reports/investment-definition-model.pdf

7

Challenging American Liberty

The Welfare State

ALREADY BEFORE *KELO*, THERE was widespread political and judicial agreement that "public use" in the Takings Clause really had the broad egalitarian meaning that was displayed in *Berman*.[1] In fact, both *Berman* and *Midkiff* redefined "public use" to include the practice of egalitarian social justice. This expansion could hardly be more explicit than in *Midkiff*, where land expropriation is approved as a means toward fighting "perceived social and economic evils". Even though the Court does not explicitly use this phrase in the *Kelo* case, by referring to *Midkiff* the Court reinforces its approval of eminent domain as a means toward advancing social justice.

To further emphasize the ideological shift in the Takings Clause, the Supreme Court has defined the term "public purpose" as synonymous with "public use". This is logical from the viewpoint of egalitarian social justice: a "purpose" is a policy goal; as demonstrated in the the discussion about the minimal state, under American liberty there can be no constitutional government functions beyond protection of life, liberty and property, and the provision of infrastructure. Therefore, a government that is limited to its constitutional functions cannot have a public purpose: the state is concentrated to the defense of citizens' private life. The only public function is in the provision of its constitutional services, which again are not public in

---

1. See: https://www.washingtonpost.com/news/volokh-conspiracy/wp/2015/05/20/my-new-book-the-grasping-hand-kelo-v-city-of-new-london-and-the-limits-of-eminent-domain/?utm_term=.b016ceee44eb

purpose. Eminent domain can be used strictly for constructing or expanding facilities for protective services, and for infrastructure.

To open up the Takings Clause in the Fifth Amendment to the practice of egalitarianism and social justice, the Supreme Court shifted the balance between government and the individual to the advantage of the former and the disadvantage of the latter. Government was given the powers to use private property as a tool for limiting individual freedom; in theory, under the "public purpose" definition eminent domain has become an instrument for the welfare state to enter any aspect of private life.

With its definition of "public purpose", the Supreme Court has granted the legislative branch, even the executive branch, the power to unilaterally define that purpose. Bluntly, the contrast between public purpose and public use is the contrast between egalitarianism and social justice on the one hand, and American liberty on the other. On the practical side of these two ideologies, this difference is the contrast between the welfare state and the minimal state. Based on *Midkiff* and *Kelo*, government could now take private property directly for the public purpose of furthering the welfare state. Technically, the link between the advancement of the ideology behind the welfare state and eminent domain is indirect: property is taken to grow the welfare state's tax base. However, the shift away from "use" to "purpose" coincides in time with the expansion of the welfare state, which in turn has drastically expanded government's need for more tax revenue.

The common name for this mechanism is "economic development". Its purpose is, squarely, to expand the tax base and thereby increase tax revenue. Not all instances of economic development use eminent domain to this effect, but all economic development aims to improve tax revenue. This point is reinforced by the reactions that followed after the Supreme Court's *Kelo* ruling.

Economic development: a tool for social justice

The *Kelo* case was driven by a clearly spelled out economic-development plan. A central part of it was to bring pharmaceutical giant Pfizer to town. The plan, which included tax breaks for the company, was compelling enough to motivate Pfizer to invest in New London.

After winning the *Kelo* case, the city of New London began clearing the Fort Trumbull area for new, private owners and property developers. For some time it looked like the city would indeed achieve its goal and expand its tax base. However, Pfizer did not stay in New London long enough for that tax base expansion to materialize. On November 12, 2009, the New York Times reported that as the company's tax breaks expired, it would close its New London facility with 1,400 jobs. As it did, it abandoned "the city's biggest office complex and an adjacent swath of barren land that was cleared of dozens of homes."[2] That swath of barren land was Fort Trumbull where Ms. Kelo and many others had once lived.

The New York Times article confirms that eminent domain was used to replace old taxpayers with new ones, i.e., "to make room for a hotel, stores and condominiums that were never built." This economic-development purpose behind the *Kelo* case is confirmed in a white paper from 2003 titled *New London Development Corporation* and published by former Connecticut College president Claire Gaudani. Ms. Gaudani was instrumental in bringing Pfizer to New London; in fact, Gaudani's paper makes clear that the *Kelo* case was all about tax-revenue growth by means of eminent domain.[3]

Since *Kelo*, governments all across America have continued to use eminent domain and, even more so, economic development. However, there has been some legislative reaction to the case, specifically with focus on limiting eminent domain. In the first year after *Kelo*, forty seven state legislatures considered bills to restrict the practice.[4] Ilya Somin, law professor at the Scalia Law School at the George Mason University, reports that as of 2015, forty five states had enacted restrictions on eminent-domain takings of private property.[5] Some of the reactions, Somin explains, were more symbolic than substantial:

> There was indeed great progress in many states. But the real achievements of the wave of eminent domain reform fell short of the appearance. In more than half of the states that enacted post-*Kelo* reform laws, the new legislation only pretended to restrict economic development takings, without actually doing so.

2. See: https://www.nytimes.com/2009/11/13/nyregion/13pfizer.html

3. The paper is a case study of economic development in Connecticut under Governor Rowland. Peggy Cosgrove is listed as having "prepared" the paper, but Claire Gaudani is its publisher. Please see: http://www.clairegaudiani.com/Writings/Writings%20PDFs/Economic%20Development%20PDFs/New%20London%20Development%20Corporation%20Case%20Study.pdf

4. See: https://www.ccim.com/sites/default/files/ccim-briefing-paper_eminent-domain.pdf

5. See: https://www.washingtonpost.com/news/volokh-conspiracy/wp/2015/06/04/the-political-and-judicial-reaction-to-kelo/?noredirect=on&utm_term=.9890749e5f81

He also reports an interesting segregation of the reactions into two categories, explainable in an ideological context:

- Reactions that originated in citizen initiatives were more in line with the principles of American liberty, trending in the libertarian direction in terms of their legislative practices;
- Reactions with legislative origin leaned egalitarian.

Somin's findings are not surprising. Incumbent legislators tend to favor budgetary status quo, meaning a gradually expanding welfare state, over reforms to limit, even shrink the size of government. Alas, under America's current welfare state it is expectable that the legislative reaction to *Kelo* is closer to the Supreme Court's public-purpose terminology than the foundations of American liberty.

Others have made a somewhat similar observation.[6] Republican-leaning states have tended toward tighter restrictions on eminent domain than Democrat-leaning states. With specific reference to economic development, Somin notes that the judicial reaction also tended in the restrictive direction. In the *Kelo* aftermath,

> the state supreme courts of Ohio, Oklahoma and South Dakota all rejected *Kelo* as a guide to the interpretation of their state constitutions' public use clauses, holding that economic development takings violated state constitutional law even if they were permissible under the Fifth Amendment.

Despite some tendencies toward a restrictive response to *Kelo*, on the balance the outcome of the case was an advancement—or at least affirmation—of economic development as a government tool to expand the tax base. The Supreme Court has left the definition of "blighted" so broadly defined, Somin explains, that "almost any neighborhood qualifies." Essentially, he says, any area that economic-development agencies set their eyes on can be "declared blighted and taken on that basis."

In the context of trends in government spending, Somin's observations are not surprising. Governments, state as well as local, have generally maxed out taxpayer tolerance toward higher taxes. To obtain more revenue, they have to chart a route forward that expands the tax base, and while there have been some applications of growth-promoting policies such as

---

6. See: https://oaktrust.library.tamu.edu/bitstream/handle/1969.1/5694/

deregulations and competitive tax cuts, it remains a popular strategy to replace lower-paying taxpayers with higher paying ones.

In terms of advancing social justice, the need for more tax revenue is unending. Economic redistribution, a.k.a., welfare-state spending, accounts for a significant and slowly growing share of state and local government outlays. For example, in 1992, states and local governments used 51.4 percent of their direct expenditures for education, social services, income maintenance, employment security, and housing. In 2016, that share had increased to 55.6 percent.

It is inherent to the welfare state to be in constant need of more tax revenue. The size of the welfare state's budget is ideologically determined, driven by the size of the population that is defined as eligible for tax-paid programs. The more people that are defined as eligible, and the more they are eligible for, the bigger is the total government budget. Spending on welfare-state programs is determined ideologically, and independently of the economic ability of taxpayers to fund those programs.

In order to protect the fiscal solvency of the welfare state, government has to constantly expand its tax base. When gradually higher taxes begin taking a toll on economic growth, as it has in most Western countries, economic development gives elected officials the perception of a tool for expanding the tax base.

Beyond the Fifth Amendment

The *Kelo* case illustrated how egalitarianism has made strides into the American constitutional republic. These strides paralleled the transformation of the welfare state from conservative to egalitarian. The ideology of social justice expanded its domain in the judicial branch in the form of a gradual re-interpretation of the protection of property rights. Likewise, social justice advanced in the form of the welfare state, in the bargain reshaping the ideological mainstream of the legislative branch. Today, to create and grow entitlement programs is no more controversial than to interpret "public use" in the Takings Clause as "public purpose".

Another parallel between the advancement of social justice in the two branches is in how our constitutional republic has responded. In both cases, the nature of the constitutional republic has put a brake pad on the wheel of egalitarian progress.

While the legislative reactions to the *Kelo* case were of mixed effectiveness in legal terms, the multitude of initiatives, and legislation, slowed down the progress of egalitarian eminent domain. When 45 states passed new laws in response to *Kelo*, as many as 90 legislative chambers had to debate and vote on them. Furthermore, the governor of each one of those states had to decide whether to approve or veto those bills.

Thanks to the fact that the United States is a federation, not a unitary state, a moderating force was applied to what could otherwise have proven to affirm, even aggravate a fairly radical change in a key part of a free society: the property right.

The welfare state provides another example of the constitutional moderating force on egalitarian progress. A welfare state that was originally created in the image of compassionate conservatism, was transformed over time to become an egalitarian structure for the advancement of social justice. However, this has not happened without the application of counterbalancing forces. Since the start of the War on Poverty—the transition point between the conservative and the egalitarian welfare states—the advancement of the egalitarian ideological project has been considerably slower than in Europe in general and Sweden in particular. There, the welfare state was built to completion in approximately 20 years; after more than half a century, the American welfare state still has not grown to completion. As of 2019 it still lacks a single-payer health care system, general income security and universal child care.

Our form of government is a major reason for the slow progress of the welfare state. With a majority-elected legislature, consisting of two chambers, and a strong, one-person executive branch with approval power for legislation and considerable policy influence, the federal government alone (not even considering the states) is equipped with substantial policy-moderating mechanisms. In terms of the welfare state, these powers have been manifested in the form of reactions to government growth, such as the tax cuts under President Reagan, welfare reform under President Clinton and, most recently, the efforts under the Trump administration to repeal parts of the Affordable Care Act.

The widespread response to the *Kelo* ruling falls into this category as well. Even if the legislative outcomes of those reactions were of mixed quality, the balance of the political response was reactionary to the egalitarian use of eminent domain. However, neither the fallout from *Kelo* nor the reforms to moderate the welfare state have halted America's slow, long-term journey in the egalitarian direction. This progress spans across the economy, with the welfare state leading the way: its promises of entitlements and of government catering to people's needs is followed by taxation and other means of raising revenue (such as economic development).

A point that is often lost in the discussion about property rights is that personal income is also property. Even though eminent domain and other laws applying to private property do not equate income to real estate, the two are similar from an economic viewpoint. Real estate provides facility for residence or the operation of a business, which in turn is a form of in-kind income. Egalitarian eminent domain makes that in-kind income conditional upon its usefulness to government; personal income, such as wages and salaries, are conditional in the same sense. Government allows income earners to keep any given share of their income that government does not deem to be needed. By the same token, a piece of real estate is not taken under egalitarian eminent domain until government deems it to be needed.

In other words, the ideological transformation of the Takings Clause bears similarities to the advancement of the same egalitarian ideology in the area of taxation. Ever since the ratification of the Sixteenth Amendment in 1913, the federal personal income tax has been used as a tool for economic redistribution. This advancement of an element of egalitarian thinking actually predates the judicial-branch advancement of social justice.

Even though the term "public purpose" is not being used in the context of taxation, it is implied in the very structure of the income tax. It is also embedded in the evolution of government spending. For example:

- In 1934 Congress passed the National Housing Act. Under a new agency, the Federal Housing Administration, the U.S. government would provide a housing safety net for the poor and those with little income.

- In 1935, the Social Security Act established the first comprehensive federal welfare program, Aid to Dependent Children (later Aid to Families with Dependent Children, renamed Temporary Assistance to Needy Families under welfare reform in 1996). That same law also created a permanent unemployment insurance program as well as the benefits commonly known under Social Security, including but not limited to retirement and disability benefits.

- In 1939 the food stamp program was born, adding yet another federally funded welfare program.

Taken together, these new functions of the federal government were the starting point of an expansion into areas outside of the duties of the minimal state. The leap into egalitarianism did not happen until 1964 and the beginning of the War on Poverty, but the programs founded in the 1930s established the notion of a public purpose for government, above and beyond its duties to protect private life. As such, the new functions led a government foray into the domain of economic redistribution and social justice.

In 1939, with the new welfare programs in place, the federal government financed a good part of its budget with highly progressive individual income taxes. There were 33 brackets in the individual income tax code, with the highest rate at 79 percent—a clear statement of intent to change the outcomes of private economic relations in the image of a public purpose.

On the spending side of the budget, these programs constituted a public purpose that was thus far limited to extensive relief for the poor and to make the wealthier Americans pay for it. No effort was made beyond that at actively redistributing income, but the creation of permanent, systematically designed, funded and operated poverty relief programs gave Congress the ideological authority to alter the outcomes of private economic activity.

The purpose of government was no longer restricted to the private sphere in people's lives—the sphere of protecting life, liberty and property and providing infrastructure. The purpose of government was now public. It was comparatively easy for the Lyndon Johnson administration and Congress to expand on the institutional structure that those programs provided, and build a welfare state that actively redistributed income and wealth between citizens.

The Marxist roots of public purpose

No writer has provided a more explicit and more elaborate definition of the term "public purpose" than Harvard economics professor John Kenneth Galbraith. In his book *Economics and the Public Purpose*, published in 1973,[7] he gave the term an explicit egalitarian economic content.

Galbraith was one of the 20th century's most prominent economists and public policy writers. He influenced several presidents and was instrumental in the design of Lyndon Johnson's War on Poverty.[8] Throughout his

---

7. Galbraith (1973).
8. Larson (2018, p. 23).

authorship he carefully elaborated on what he saw as the systemic flaws in American capitalism, flaws that his contributions to policy reform were aimed at correcting. He made the term "public purpose" the common analytical denominator of his policy reform agenda.

John Rawls and J K Galbraith were of the same ideological conviction. Both were egalitarians and favored extensive, social-justice driven economic redistribution. They also complemented one another: where Rawls was a theorist, Galbraith was the policy engineer who brought egalitarian ideas from the armchair to the legislature. He was more influential on U.S. economic and social policy in the 20th century than any other individual; perhaps his most lasting achievement was to assist President Lyndon Johnson in transforming the American welfare state from a conservative safety net to a structure for the advancement of the egalitarian ideology.

Galbraith defined the public purpose as being one of conflict resolution, but not in disagreements between individuals. Like Rawls, Galbraith saw a free society and its free economy as inherently conflict-ridden. To Rawls,

- one man's liberty could only expand at the expense of another's;
- with liberty inextricably tied to economic means, the distribution of income becomes essential to the distribution of liberty.

To secure equal liberty for all, Rawls prescribed far-reaching economic redistribution. Galbraith explained how that would happen, but instead of trying to tie social justice to liberty, he centered his analysis entirely around a Marxist definition of power. In concentrate, this means that Galbraith saw the public purpose of the state as intervening in a struggle to control the means of production. Plainly, this leads to the same policy conclusion as in Rawls: systemic intervention by the state into the distribution of income between labor and capital.

The idea that there is a conflict over income redistribution is entirely Marxist in nature:

- Labor is responsible for the entire value of production: it is the factory worker's hands that assembles manufactured products; the construction worker's hands build houses; the farmer's hands bring in the harvest;
- Capital owns the means of production and therefore claims part of the so-called surplus value from production.

Marxist theory splits business sales revenue into two parts. First, there is the subsistence wage, or the minimum amount of money that the worker needs in order to reproduce his own work. In practical terms, it is the food, shelter, clothing and transportation that the worker needs to be able to come back the next day and repeat the production process. Then there is the surplus value, which is the difference between sales revenue and the total amount of subsistence wages paid out to workers. Conventionally, this amount is referred to as the profit of the business.

To the Marxist, the distribution of sales revenue between subsistence wages and profits represents a distribution of economic power. He equates distribution of power to distribution of income in much the same way as Rawls equates distribution of liberty to distribution of income. The difference is that Marxist theory of power is about income as it is earned in production, while Rawls's theory of justice is about economic outcomes. In essence, this is the difference between the distribution of income earned and the distribution of purchasing power.

The alleged conflict is straightforwardly laid out in Marxist literature. Suppose a worker spends ten hours per day at an assembly line. To use entirely hypothetical numbers, the total sales revenue from a day's worth of production is $10, or $1 per hour. Suppose the subsistence wage, as defined by Marxist theory, is $3 per day; the surplus from production is $7. (Marxists conventionally disregard inputs, taxes and other costs for operating a business.) If there is no redistribution of income, each worker will have $3 to spend while the owner of the business will have $7 per worker.

In a real free-market, capitalist economy, workers do not make subsistence wages. Their earnings are considerably higher. An egalitarian welfare state, however, changes the notion of subsistence by redefining it. While Marx gave it an absolute meaning—the means to survive and work another day—modern welfare states rely instead on a relative definition. Specifically, the definition of poverty that underpins federally sponsored welfare programs in today's America, is such that the actual meaning of "being poor" changes with the general growth in standard of living. A person is poor when he earns a certain percentage of median income; when median income rises, the actual monetary value of poverty rises as well.

The relative definition of poverty serves a distinct ideological purpose, namely to neutralize the effects of time on economic differences. When an economy grows, it elevates the standard of living of the entire population. It is not the case that people in every income layer will experience the same increase—for some income may go up more than for others—but over time the standard of living rises across the economy. It is not meaningful to say that anyone lives in subsistence today in the same way as they did when Marx authored his economic theory in the mid-19th century.

Since the conditions of the working poor—notwithstanding government aid—have changed radically over the long term, the case for economic redistribution, as defined by Marx, no longer exists. The relative definition of poverty serves the purpose of maintaining the Marxist conflict over income redistribution. To put it in those terms: the concept of relative poverty gives the impression that over time, capitalists continuously try to suppress worker earnings, keeping them at a subsistence standard of living, in order to maximize the surplus value, i.e., profits.

With the distribution of income from production being equal to the distribution of economic power, Marxist theory suggests, the alleged, sustained suppression of wages by capitalists is the same as suppression of workers' power. Therefore, Marxists draw far-reaching policy conclusions from their theory, conclusions that fall into two categories.

The first category is revolutionary, demanding the termination of capitalism and its system of property rights. Workers should seize factories, either by armed revolution or by socializing property through legislation. Either way, the goal is to end free-market capitalism as a socio-economic system and replace it with egalitarianism.

This category focuses on changing the distribution of income from production. The idea is that if workers—represented by a state which in turn is run by a Marxist party—seize the means of production, they will get to keep the entire surplus value.

The second policy category is reformist. Instead of eliminating property rights, reformists seek to change the distribution of income after it has been determined in production but before it defines the worker's bottom line. This category leads to well-known features of modern, redistributive government: a progressive income tax that takes an increasing share of a person's income as it goes up, coupled with a system of entitlement programs that provides cash or in-kind services to lower-earning families.

By means of this redistributive system—the welfare state—government alters economic outcomes that Marxists and Rawlsian egalitarians otherwise define as unequal or unjust. The ties between economic redistribution and, respectively, liberty (Rawls) and power (Marx, Galbraith) create a political imperative for economic redistribution that goes beyond the income and wealth that individual citizens may or may not have. Those ties politicize the earnings of every citizen, as well as his standard of living.

Every person's earnings become a matter of public purpose, either in the form of eligibility for entitlements or as subject of taxation to fund those entitlements. Progressive taxation and welfare-state spending become reformist instruments to redistribute power over society from one group of citizens to another.

Galbraith is a reformist in this sense—he explicitly rejects the revolutionary alternative—seeing the welfare state as a structure for redistribution of income, consumption and power.

It is not clear from Galbraith's writings what exactly it means to hold power in proportion to economic resources.[9] Power is a relation where one person can coercively influence another person's overall behavior, or at least individual actions.[10] The implication from Marxist theory is that people who control large corporations can exercise power over what products people buy, from cars and appliances to phone services and health care. However, in a free society the consumer is autonomous in that he will not buy a Ford over a Hyundai because the Ford family is very wealthy. He will choose his vehicle based on its properties and how those are relevant to his needs and preferences.

Power, the Marxist will suggest, is exercised more subtly, as in advertising and attempts by big corporations to monopolize markets, thereby restricting consumer choice. However, in a free, modern economy where there are no entry or exit barriers to markets—imposed by government regulations—competition and the pursuit of profit do a fair job of keeping product supply and choice at levels appealing to consumers in general. There will never be the perfect market as depicted in economics textbooks, but, again in a free society, there will also never be the confinement of the Marxist-theorized capitalist monopoly.

The only way that economic wealth creates a sword to wield power over people's lives is through undue influence over government. If, and only if, government gets into the habit of selectively favoring some industries

---

9. Galbraith (2010).

10. There is a plethora of literature on power, spanning a number of social-science disciplines: political economy, political science, history, psychology and assorted ad-hoc examples. To cover this literature in the context of the present analysis would be to force the reader onto a tangent demanding considerable time for very little value added. However, all studies of power share one common denominator: "power" is differentiated from "influence" by a coercive component. This denominator is a sufficient definition for the present discourse.

and businesses at the expense of others, will economic wealth lead to the consequences predicted by Marxist theory.

Furthermore, if power is tied to economic means, then individuals in the United States today are far more powerful than they were a century ago. As the standard of living rises, so would people's power. Marxist theory escapes the logic in this point by assuming, again, that power is a zero-sum game. If the capitalist has more, the worker has less. Logically, this necessitates a conclusion on their behalf that economic resources are also absolutely finite; economic growth as a means to prosperity is either irrelevant or futile.

That is not to say that Galbraith—a distinguished economist—dismissed growth. He shared the same understanding for the need for economic growth as many of his contemporary representatives of the intellectual left. The point, however, is that in the choice between policies that promote economic growth and those that redistribute income among the citizenry, Galbraith squarely came down on the side of redistribution.

His motivation for prioritizing economic redistribution is to be found in his reliance on Marxism. Having rejected revolution as a means toward a completely egalitarian society, Galbraith was left with the reformist path to a fully-fledged welfare state. By Marxist terminology, government could only redistribute power through comprehensive economic redistribution.

Social justice at work

From the vantage point of power, Galbraith thinks of the state's public purpose as a reformist toolkit for creating a new balance between labor and capital. Galbraith explains the need for changing the balance with the evolution that the economic system has undergone since the birth of capitalism.

With modern industrial production and the shareholder system of corporate ownership, capitalism created two distinctly different spheres in the economy. One sphere, says Galbraith, is where households and small entrepreneurs operate; the other is home to capitalists and executives of large corporations. Galbraith calls the former the "market system", while the latter is oddly named the "planning system".

The reason why Galbraith refers to large corporations as a planned part of the economy is that large corporations operate on terms of economic planning, committing resources, setting prices and managing purchases, marketing and production on multi-year schedules. In planning their activities, Galbraith suggests, corporations impose their long-term plans on consumers, employees and smaller entrepreneurs who lack the long-term planning ability of large corporations.[11]

His distinction between the market system and the planning system is a picture of the distribution of power over the economy. Households and small businesses have little power; large corporations have considerable power. Galbraith exemplifies this power imbalance in the context of what he refers to as the "technostructure". For a long time, he explains, technological innovation was "an absolute social good" that only "eccentrics" questioned. It was even a virtuous function of government to promote innovation and scientific progress. However, he suggests, over time big corporations have increasingly adopted the behavior of capitalists as they are depicted in Marxist literature:[12]

> Now doubt is commonplace. Much innovation in consumers' goods is felt to be fraudulent. It is taken for granted that many much-heralded inventions will have as their most striking feature that they do not work or they will prove hazardous. ... And increasingly it is believed of innovation that, though it serves its function—though it moves people ad supersonic speeds or destroys incoming missiles—it is impressively negligent of the consequent social damage or public danger.

Galbraith's point is that under large corporations—within the so-called planning system—technological innovation serves the purposes of corporations rather than consumers. Without going into too much detail on the nature of the technostructure, Galbraith ignores the good that technological progress has done for mankind. Medical technology today allows for the saving of lives far beyond what people could have imagined even a century ago. Computer technology has connected the world, elevated productivity, expanded moral, social and cultural horizons and even helped

---

11. Since smaller economic agents operate with smaller resources, the theory is that they have a shorter term of commitment and therefore are closer to a free market in their behavior. This, however, is incorrect. An individual making minimum wage has the same need to be able to predict his costs and his spending margins as a large, multi-billion dollar corporation. In fact, the low-wage earner lives within tighter financial margins and therefore has a stronger need for predictability and—as a logical consequence—planning of his resources, than a corporation with considerable financial resources at its disposal. Therefore, the use of the term "planning system" is misplaced.

12. See Galbraith (1973, p. 142).

advance freedom by undermining totalitarian regimes. In the past 50 years alone, manufacturing technology has lowered the cost of consumer goods and other basic conveniences of life, making affordable everything from indoor plumbing and other sanitary functions to telephones, home appliances, computers, even cars. In the past 50 years, technological advancements have elevated more than two billion people around the world from abject poverty to at least a moderate standard of modern living.

Yet the criticism from Galbraith, classic as it is in egalitarian circles, serves a distinct Marxist purpose. It is based on the notion that our economy relies on a culture of "consumerism" where corporations exercise power over consumers by forcing them to lead a life they would allegedly otherwise not have chosen. Their goals, Galbraith contends, are not the goals of the public. On the contrary, corporations, in the form of the so-called planning system, "will continue to pursue its purposes under the protection of the belief that its goals are those that best serve the public" (p. 213). Ignoring the fact that businesses do not prevail if consumers do not like their products, Galbraith sees a discord between business purposes and the needs and preferences of their customers. This discord is yet another iteration of the struggle for power between labor and capital—hence Galbraith's inevitable ideological conclusion: government has a public purpose in neutralizing the power of corporations.

Galbraith divides this public purpose into three parts:

1. Income redistribution, primarily through union power. Galbraith does not offer explicit reform ideas, but he hints of legislation that strengthens unions vs. corporations. This usually means termination of right-to-work freedom and other means to give unions a coercive position—power—to demand higher compensation independently of what a business can actually afford.

2. A form of microeconomic planning to secure that government resources "serve not the planning system but the public". This consists of urban planning, including but not limited to aggressive use of zoning laws, to curtail so-called overdevelopment; environmental regulations; and "making technology serve public and not technocratic interest" (p. 214). Galbraith does not specify this last point; ostensibly, he refers to heavy regulations of prices and investments within telecommunications and similar industries.

3. Indicative, macroeconomic planning. Galbraith's non-exhaustive list of examples includes:

   a. providing housing, infrastructure and mass transit, health care and performing arts services;

   b. income redistribution beyond what stronger unions can achieve, in the form of progressive income taxes and redistributive entitlements; and

   c. "inter-industry coordination".

In other words, it is the public purpose of government to build a welfare state based on egalitarian social-justice principles.

In a succinct summary, Galbraith outlines how a government behaves that does not promote the public purpose (p. 283):

> The government, we have seen, contributes notably to inequality in development. Where the industry is powerful, government responds strongly to its needs. And also to its products. It gives the automobile industry roads for its cars, the weapons industry orders for its weapons, other industries support for research and development. By the same token it is sparing in its support to the weaker parts of the planning system, more so to the market system, most of all to public need unrelated to economic interest.

More to the point, he explains:

> As this book goes to press, support for agriculture, housing, education, health and the poor is being reduced by a Republican administration because of a need to economize and because also of the low cost-effectiveness of these programs. Despite peace and the avowed need to economized, and with no claims for their cost-effectiveness, defense expenditures are being increased.

Herein, Galbraith spells out the policy content of government's public purpose. All the functions listed under cuts are functions that are directly or indirectly redistributive in nature. Government provides services for lower-income segments of the population, paid for with taxes that disproportionately burden higher incomes.

The public purpose is the advancement of egalitarianism, i.e., of social justice.

8

Social Justice vs. American Liberty

WHEN SOCIAL JUSTICE ADVANCES, it entrenches itself in the institutions of government, the economy and society as a whole. It rewrites the purpose of government and demotes the individual to an instrument for public policy.

The transformation of a society from a minimal state to a welfare state goes through three distinct phases.

Upon completion, the transformation has replaced American liberty with totalitarianism.

Three phases of ideological transformation

It would be wrong to state that the United States Constitution represents a perfect origin for libertarianism. It fails to provide an unequivocal bulwark against economic redistribution—hence the rise of the egalitarian welfare state—and it leaves many elements of state-individual interaction open to interpretation. In fairness, the concept of economic redistribution was relatively unknown in the late 18th century; its evolution to political relevance took place a century after the signing of the Constitution. Understandably, the Founding Fathers did not see an imminent need to shield the new constitutional republic from such ideas.

Furthermore, despite its shortcomings the founding document of the American constitutional republic is as close as one could have expected it to be, given the time and circumstances of its writing. It is at least a reasonable representation of a practical point of origin for libertarian ideology.

At this, libertarianism was not complete but as comprehensive as it could become, given the circumstances of that time. Institutionalized discrimination such as slavery and the barring of Catholics from participating in politics were done away with as the republic evolved. It goes without saying that if a constitutional republic would take shape today, its libertarian character traits would be stronger.

Therefore, the point of origin—point (1)—in Figure 2 below is to be understood as a generalization, not an absolute representation, of the libertarian origin. As the American constitutional republic evolved, it began trading liberty (the blue line for social justice (red). This trade-off has strict economic terms; again, the liberation of slaves, the introduction of universal suffrage and end to religious discrimination represented important advances in libertarianism. As welcome as they were, they did not represent any evolution in the ideological competition over the institutional design of our economy.

In short, Figure 2 is limited in its scope to how the advance of social justice gradually claims monopoly on defining America's socio-economic character.

Figure 2

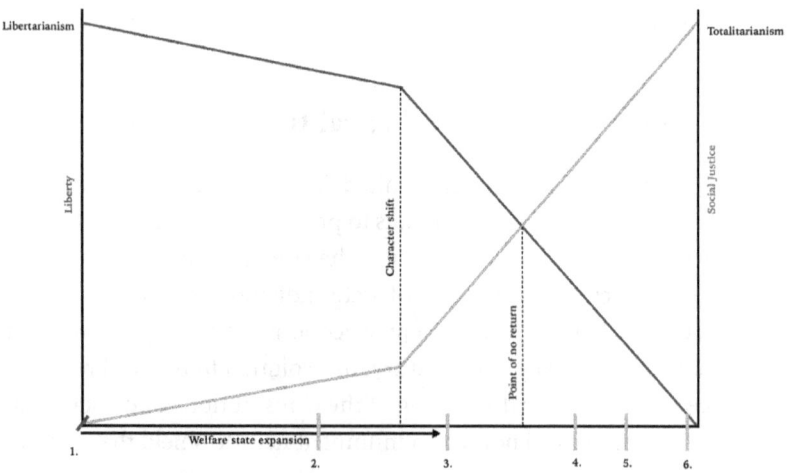

As social justice advances over time, it gradually trades place with libertarianism as the ideology defining the United States. For a long time, the transformation was slow, represented by crawling growth in limited welfare programs and government participation in the economy. In the early 20th century, represented by point (2), a progressive federal income tax under President Taft was followed by a set of poverty-relieving welfare programs under President Franklin Roosevelt.

With the War on Poverty, the American welfare state changed character. The absolute definition of poverty was replaced with a new, relative definition that refocused the entire welfare state: its purpose was no longer to provide last-resort relief for poverty, but to permanently redistribute income. Once this point was passed, the welfare state was actively advancing social justice at the expense of liberty; with the growth of entitlement programs such as (but not limited to) food stamps, subsidized housing, Medicaid and the Earned Income Tax Credit the ideology of social justice rapidly grew to prominence in defining America's character.

As government expands its presence in the economy, its need for tax revenue has grown. Over time, the progressive nature of our federal income-tax system has grown to a point where approximately one quarter of all individual taxpayers pay 80 percent of all personal federal income taxes. After the Trump tax reform of 2018 this group provides approximately two thirds of total federal tax revenue.[1]

The combination of progressive taxes and the advancement of judicial egalitarianism (as exemplified by the *Kelo* case) have contributed to the acccelerated phase-out of libertarianism and phase-in of social justice. America's character shift has progressed rapidly since the beginning of the War on Poverty, placing us close to (3), but not beyond the point of no return.

Only a small number of new entitlement programs are needed to push America past the point of no return:

- A single-payer health care system would reconfigure our health care system in the image of egalitarian social justice: the provision of medical services would be conditioned upon criteria for equal distribution of available resources—not health care itself—and denials of care based primarily on cost, not medical outcomes;

- A general income security system, spearheaded by paid family leave, would make it more affordable for families to remain in lower-income jobs while increasing the relative cost of earning high incomes as benefits would be capped at moderate income levels; taxes would also increase disproportionately on higher incomes, further reinforcing the

---

1. See Larson (2018a).

social-justice character of our welfare state; the welfare state would also expand its presence in our economy by virtue of providing this new entitlement—replacing the need for private savings for income security;

- A universal child-care system would enroll all children in day care and preschool programs funded, run and curricularly defined by government; child care would change from a private matter into an area for the advancement of social justice.

Once a country transitions past the point of no return, it progresses with relative speed toward the end of the scale. Figure 3 explains this point in more detail.

Figure 3

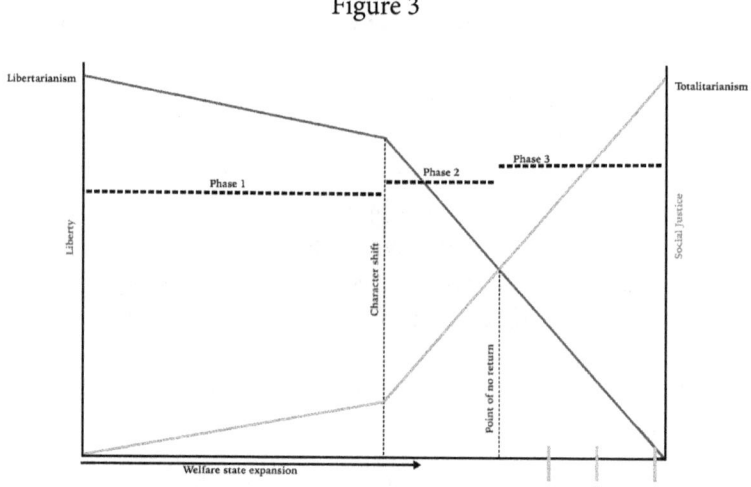

During Phase 1 the welfare state is restricted to a last-resort function for those who have no other means to provide for themselves. In Phase 2 the welfare state has changed character; by means of its growing presence in the economy it is rapidly changing the character of the nation as a whole.

Phase 3 begins when the welfare state has been completed to include full government control over health care, child care, income security, education, retirement and other aspects of family life that can be politicized short of a totalitarian government. Once the welfare state has reached this point, a nation's libertarian character traits will have been reduced to residual pockets within a socio-economic structure that is otherwise entirely egalitarian.

In our modern world, there are many examples of countries that have transitioned from Phase 2 to Phase 3. Sweden, at point (4), is one. It only took that country some 20 years to pass through Phase 2; institutionally, the Swedish welfare state was complete at the end of the 1950s. As explained earlier, its culture and social character has been entrenched in the egalitarian welfare state since at least the 1970s.

Greece represents a welfare state that has moved further into Phase 2 (point 5). After its severe austerity crisis in the early 2010s, the Hellenic nation has been economically diminished and politically and socially bogged down in a welfare state that it can no longer afford.[2] Sweden is in the same position but has been able to keep its welfare state in somewhat better shape; the difference between the two countries is, however, more a matter of time than character.

Eventually, a welfare state continues its transformation of a nation's character, to the point where libertarianism is nowhere to be found (point 6). The more compelling contemporary example of the welfare state's totalitarian end-point is Venezuela. At the point of completion of this book manuscript, that country is on the brink of political chaos, following years of progressing economic implosion. It is important, however, to recognize that the decline of Venezuela began in the late 1990s as an accelerated experiment with a full-fledged egalitarian welfare state. Where Sweden transitioned through Phase 2 in only 20 years, Venezuela passed through Phase 3 about as fast.

Once the welfare state has transitioned out of Phase 1, it becomes increasingly difficult to reverse its progress. Social justice entrenches itself in the socio-economic organization, defining our political and economic institutions to a point where ideological alternatives seem unrealistic, even inconceivable. During Phase 2, it is still possible to reverse the welfare state into Phase 1, but as the following example shows, the political, legislative and judicial obstacles are almost insurmountable.

---

2. See Larson (2018b).

Texas v Azar

Obamacare, also known as the Affordable Care Act (ACA), is one of the most apparent examples of how entitlement programs are rarely reversed. From its election win in 2016 to its loss of the House of Representatives in 2018, the Republican party spent a considerable amount of legislative time and effort trying to decide what to do with President Obama's signature addition to the welfare state. The only outcome of those deliberations was a repeal of the individual mandate to buy health insurance, allowing individuals to be uninsured without risking a penalty.

Disregarding the legal aspects of the ACA—some of which have already been played out in the Supreme Court—the ideology behind the law is the same as is behind every advancement of the egalitarian welfare state. The ACA is redistributive in nature, giving health-insurance premium subsidies to individuals and families with low incomes, while using revenue from a progressive tax system to fund those subsidies. Alas, designed to advance social justice, the ACA is ideologically incompatible with the U.S. Constitution. This is in fact spelled out in the design of the law, which is made constitutional entirely through the ability of Congress to levy taxes.

In short: Congress had an ambition to advance social justice; the U.S. Constitution does not give government an apparent way to do so; to still be able to advance social justice, Congress formulated the law so that it would fit a part of the constitution that was not intentionally designed for that very purpose. The taxation power, which anchors the ACA in our nation's founding document, is granted Congress under the Sixteenth Amendment. Since this Amendment does not spell out any limitations on how Congress can use its taxation powers, Congress has over the years created a precedent—an interpretation of the Amendment—where any use of tax revenue is constitutional so long as that revenue has been collected in compliance with the Amendment.

Then came *Texas v Azar*:[3]

> In a 55-page opinion, U.S. District Judge Reed O'Connor ruled that last year's tax cut bill knocked the constitutional foundation from under "Obamacare" by eliminating a penalty for not having coverage. The rest of the law cannot be separated from that provision and is therefore invalid, he wrote.

---

3. See: https://www.denverpost.com/2018/12/14/texas-federal-judge-obama-health-care-law-unconstitutional/

As explained in the meaty part of the ruling, it was Congress that created the very tool that put Obamacare in existential jeopardy:[4]

> [Sometimes], a court must determine whether the Constitution grants Congress the power it asserts and what results if it does not. If a party shows that a policymaker exceeded the authority granted it by the Constitution, the fruit of that unauthorized action cannot stand.

In other words, the Constitution does not permit economic redistribution per se (which is what Obamacare really is all about). In its ambition to advance the ideology of social justice, Congress has asserted its power to redistribute and constitutionally anchored it in its power to tax. It is implied that because of its taxation power, Congress can use its revenue however it wants to. It is this very assertion that was the focal point of *Texas v Azar*. Specifically, says the syllabus of the case,

> the Plaintiffs allege that, following passage of the Tax Cuts and Jobs Act of 2017 (TCJA), the Individual Mandate in the Patient Protection and Affordable Care Act (ACA) is unconstitutional. They say it is no longer fairly readable as an exercise of Congress's Tax Power and continues to be unsustainable under the Interstate Commerce Clause.

The Sixteenth Amendment has no limitations as to how Congress can spend its tax revenue. This omission of a preemptive mechanism barring economic redistribution resembles the omission of such restrictions in the Constitution itself. The reason for such omissions is likely the same in both cases: the idea of a welfare state of modern proportions was incomprehensible at the time. This, however, has allowed proponents of social justice to interpret that omission as a blank check on government spending: what is not specifically prohibited is permitted.

In effect, this has allowed Congress to place the entire welfare state in the Constitution by means of the Sixteenth Amendment. Over the decades, Congress has created countless entitlement programs, from Social Security in the 1930s to SCHIP in the 1990s, all of which are incompatible with ideological foundation of the Constitution.

As a matter of fact, *Texas v Azar* exposes this constitutional anchor by referring back to a Supreme Court case, *NFIB v Sebelius*, that determined

---

4. See: https://oag.ca.gov/system/files/attachments/press-docs/211-texas-order-granting-plaintiffs-partial-summary-judgment.pdf?rel=0

the status of Obamacare. The Court rules that the individual insurance-purchase mandate of Obamacare

> was unconstitutional under the Interstate Commerce Clause but could fairly be read as an exercise of Congress's Tax Power because it triggered a tax. The TCJA eliminated that tax. The Supreme Court's reasoning in NFIB — buttressed by other binding precedent and plain text — thus compels the conclusion that the Individual Mandate may no longer be upheld under the Tax Power. And because the Individual Mandate continues to mandate the purchase of health insurance, it remains unsustainable under the Interstate Commerce Clause — as the Supreme Court already held.

This is important. The question here is not whether Congress can redistribute money between individual citizens. The question is how Congress can do so constitutionally. In effect, *NFIB* and *Azar* put on full display the ideological contrast between the United States Constitution and the welfare state as represented by the Affordable Care Act.

Inherent conflict: the iron law of wages

As the political and judicial battle over Obamacare is a good example of the ideological incompatibility of the welfare state and the U.S. Constitution, it shares a fundamental character trait with the erosion of the eminent-domain tool under the Fifth Amendment, namely that government imposes its ideological preference for economic outcomes upon the free market and free society.

Both these examples also illustrate how social justice as an ideology cannot fit inside the Constitution. Every attempt at making that happen results in a hybrid solution where the constitutional protection of liberty is eroded. This is no coincidence, but the result of a common denominator for all iterations of social-justice policy. That common denominator is Marxist conflict theory.

Rawls provided the ideological approval of the welfare state, i.e., the state the interests of which rank higher than the interests of the individual citizen. Galbraith provided its economic imperative. Both of them rely on a common foundation of Marxist economic theory, which—again—is a theory of conflict. According to Marx, the economic system we know as free-market capitalism is characterized by inherent conflicts over finite economic resources. The part about finite resources is not contestable: in fact, the very definition of an economy is that it is a system for satisfaction of needs by means of scarce resources, subject to uncertainty.

What is subject to challenge is the conflict element and the notion that the finite supply of resources in the economy is also static. Both Rawls and Galbraith take Marx's conflict premise for granted; the assumption of static resources takes a different but comparable format. In Rawls' theory of social justice, liberty is a commodity that can never be increased, only redistributed; in Galbraith's economic theory, the distribution of income is a matter of power over the means of production. One man's liberty can only be expanded at the expense of the liberty of another man; likewise, one man's income can only increase at the cost of diminishing another man's income.

Both Rawls and Galbraith advocate one form or another of government distribution of the resource of their focus. Rawls can only make his theory work under a panel of government experts that determine one moral theory—one ideology—for society as a whole; only then can government guarantee that liberty, as he defines it, is distributed as Rawls' egalitarian ideology prescribes. Likewise, Galbraith's theory of new socialism can only impose a public purpose, i.e., a form of economic redistribution, upon society under a system of indicative economic planning. Income distribution is no longer a matter of the free market; a panel of experts are charged with *re*-distributing income according to egalitarian principles.

The common denominator of inherent conflict over a given resource in Rawlsian ethics and Galbraithian economics, prescribes that public policy should not be concerned with either economic growth or individual freedom. What matters instead is the relative position of each individual citizen in the forms of liberty and income. Since Rawls defines liberty in economic terms, the conflict according to both him and Galbraith is one over income distribution.

When an ideology rests on the premise of inherent conflict, it pays little to no attention to economic growth. In fact, much of today's political left in America has adopted this Marxist view of growth.[5] Instead, proponents of social justice pay all their attention to the conflict over income distribution, a conflict they cannot solve without clashing with the values underpinning the Constitution. As noted previously, there is a fundamental difference

---

5. Larson (2018, ch. 6).

between the libertarian view of human nature and its counterpart under the egalitarian ideology:

- Robert Nozick suggests that men generally obey laws and thereby keep society both free and peaceful;
- John Rawls characterizes man as a rational egoist, whose pursuit of his own goal runs into inevitable conflict over the scarce resource of liberty.

The tie breaker, again, is God: since God is not an egoist, He has not created us in his image as egoists. Since we are not egoists by nature, the society we build is not one of inherent conflict. It is, instead, in our nature to solve conflicts through voluntary interaction and economic exchange.

Since God is the tie breaker, when He is removed from any analysis of our society, it becomes difficult to explain human society as an evolving project, improved upon over time by every new generation. It is easy to see human imperfections over virtues, and to see those imperfections as static character traits rather than elements in dynamic human evolution. Furthermore, in the absence of God there is no scale against which to measure human character traits. Self-interested behavior is easily interpreted as egoism, simply because there is no independent way to give man a reason to rise above egoism.

God gives man a reason to do so: in His image, we strive to become better, more perfect (though never perfect) individuals. Since God is compassionate, we strive to become more compassionate; when we strive to become more compassionate, we refute egoism. In God's absence, compassion is not an apparent human character trait; without compassion, self interest becomes egoism.

Rawls defines man as a rational egoist. Since egoists act to further their own interests with indifference to interpersonal consequences of such behavior, it is natural to define a society populated by rational egoists as a society of inherent conflicts. The Marxist theory of conflict provides the foundation that both Rawls and Galbraith need for their endorsements of egalitarianism and social justice.

The core of Marxist theory, called the iron law of wages, fits neatly into a narrative of social and economic conflict, and provides the theoretical framework for why the only solution to that conflict is economic redistribution. The theory of the iron law of wages also explains why the ideology of social justice necessarily prescribes policy solutions that are unconstitutional—to a degree even anti-constitutional.

Originally formulated by economist David Ricardo in his book *On the Principles of Political Economy and Taxation*, this law defines two kinds of wages:

- The market wage, which is what workers are paid depending on the actual conditions of the labor market in terms of supply and demand; and
- The natural wage, which is what workers need to make in order to sustain themselves.

The dynamic between the natural wage and the market wage is the source of the conflict that Marxism exploits for political purposes.

The natural wage represents an existential minimum where workers can afford to eat, have a roof over their heads and keep themselves in good basic health. It is absolute in that it is determined by man's basic biological needs, which do not change much over time.

The dynamic of the iron law of wages lies in the contrast between the market wage and the natural wage. In deep recessions the former declines toward, even equals the latter; however, under regular labor market conditions, workers earn a market wage that exceeds the natural wage. In growth periods, the market wage again exceeds the natural wage, but the cyclical variations are less important than the long-term dynamic between the natural and market wages. It is over time that technological innovation, by generating increases in labor productivity, permanently raises the market wage above the natural wage. As a result of the growing gap, the overall standard of living increases. It is not the case that advancements in prosperity will spread evenly across the economy, but the long-term trend will be one of increasingly higher standard of living. Today, the industrialized world enjoys a far more prosperous and comfortable life than the same countries did in the 19th century.

So far, the theory of natural and market wages is nothing controversial. The seed of conflict is planted when Ricardo places a Malthusian restriction on the market-wage driven rise in economic well-being. As people enjoy a higher standard of living, he theorizes, the rate of successful procreation increases; people have more babies that survive infancy. As a result, population bounces up against what Ricardo defines as a fixed resource: food supply—or, more specifically, the supply of arable land. Similarly, but not to the same absolute degree, land available for housing is increasingly scarce. As a result, prices on basic necessities such as food and housing rise. This inflation, which has an approximate counterpart in modern parlance under "core inflation", diminishes the margin between the natural wage and the market wage. Eventually, according to Ricardo, the natural wage catches up with the market wage, eliminating the economic surplus that caused the population growth. People's standard of living is knocked back to where it was prior to the rise in the market wage.

So far, there is nothing controversial with the iron law, except perhaps its inability to withstand the test of time. Technically, all that Ricardo's version of the law says, is that it is futile for workers to try to advance their standard of living under capitalism. However, in fairness to Ricardo, he formulated the law as an experiment in economic theory, explaining the interaction of variables in the free market over the long term. The theory does not explicitly exclude advances in technology, worker skills and other variables that allow a permanent gap between the market wage and the natural wage. The idea that no such gap is possible is instead the brainchild of Karl Marx. His version of the iron law of wages—a distortionary adaptation of Ricardo's original—reformulated it as a theory of power struggle and conflict.

The Marxist version does not define a natural wage, but a "subsistence" wage. Its function is essentially the same: workers make enough to survive but nothing more. Survival, again, is defined as "reproduction" of the labor force.

Marx also imports the concept of a market wage, which he defines essentially in the same way as Ricardo does. This gives the Marxist iron law the same basic dynamic properties as the Ricardian version. The difference is in what forces Marx sees as creating the gap between the market wage and the subsistence wage—and what forces can prevent that gap.

Here, Marx turns to income distribution. The value of production, he says, is distributed between labor and capital, and there is only one force that determines the distribution: the success with which the capitalist suppresses the labor share. In other words, Marx removes the market forces that Ricardo relies on for his long-term analysis of the iron law. Where Ricardo analyzes the interaction between supply and demand, Marx confines the forces of market-wage suppression to the capitalist's efforts to maximize his share of the production value.

The capitalist, in Marx's eyes, is a rational egoist who is indifferent to the well-being of his workers. All he is worried about is profit, which Marx defines as the production value that exceeds the subsistence wage. It follows that Marxism defines efforts to increase capital-based income as "profit maximization". This definition is not consistent with the standard theory of economics, but it creates a communicating vessel between Marxist theory and the political pursuit of social justice. The capitalist, namely, strives to maximize profits by means of pushing down the market wage toward the subsistence wage. He does this with an "army" of unemployed workers. When wages rise above the subsistence level, Marxist theory dictates that capitalists cause a recession by laying off workers. When unemployment is high enough, they hire new workers from the ranks of the unemployed. Excess labor supply vouches for a subsistence price—subsistence wage—for labor. As businesses grow and the economic impact of each of them expands, capitalists will try to keep a permanent "army" of unemployed.

This is, in a nutshell, the Marxist version of the iron law of wages. Its main contribution is in Marx's replacing Ricardo's exogenous restraints on growth with a conflict between labor and capital. Marx trivializes the market forces that cause wages to rise and fall with the ebb and flow of the free market. Instead, he endogenizes the gap between the subsistence (natural) wage and the market wage by placing power over income distribution in the hands of capitalists.

Hence the power discussion that leads Galbraith to define a public purpose for government.

Foundations of the welfare state: the relative definition of poverty

Under the Ricardian definition of the iron law of wages, workers can rise out of poverty thanks to technological innovation, productivity gains, educational attainment and free-market competition for capital and labor. Poverty remains a constant state of existence, thus becoming increasingly irrelevant as economic growth elevates the economy to increasingly advanced levels of prosperity.

Under the Marxist version of the law, poverty is also a constant state, but the worker's only way out of it is blocked by the capitalist. There is no path to prosperity through economic growth. Herein lies the source of the egalitarian indifference to growth as well as the conclusion by both Rawls and Galbraith that only economic redistribution offers the worker a path to a better life. This path is paved with either of two political methods:

- the revolutionary elimination of private property, or
- the reformist combination of progressive taxes on higher incomes—attempting to capture what Marx defined as "profits"—and increasingly generous entitlements.

Egalitarian welfare states in the Western world have followed the second route. Their base is the notion that only government can elevate the working class above subsistence living. In other words, those who are entitled to help from the welfare state are eligible precisely because capitalism, according to Marxist doctrine, traps them in permanent subsistence living—in other words, a life in poverty.

Over time, Marxists have even learned to overcome the challenge that reality has presented to their theory. When dramatic gains in technological innovation, productivity, skills and education, allowed the working class to climb far above subsistence living, proponents of economic redistribution simply chose to redefine the meaning of subsistence living. This would address the empirical problem they saw in a working class that moved out of squalor into their own homes, drove new cars, clothed their children with decency, ate nutritious food and could afford a number of quality items and experiences in daily life, from the telephone and the television to vacation trips. As a result, there would no longer be any need for a welfare state. The capitalist had become wealthier, but so had the worker.

As time proved Ricardo right and Marx wrong, disciples of Marx found a remedy in redefining poverty. A person was no longer considered poor if his living conditions were at an absolute subsistence level; poverty became a relative condition. A person is poor if his income is of a certain percentage of median income in the economy.

Since the beginning of the War on Poverty, this relative definition is also official policy of the U.S. government.[6] The income levels that determine poverty are adjusted annually based on changes in the Consumer Price Index (the most common measurement of inflation). In practice, this construction secures annual updates proximate to the progress in general

---

6. For an example of how the U.S. government altered the definition of poverty, see Larson (2018, ch. 2).

household income. Poverty becomes a matter of a relative standard of living, not absolute subsistence.[7]

With the relative definition of poverty from 1964 and its substantial revision in 1969, the income that constituted the federal poverty limit would rise more or less on par with household income. In theory, the relative poverty definition pegs the poverty level at 60 percent of median household income; in practice, due to calculation methods the ratio is not straightforward against standard definitions of median income. The grey line in Figure 4 reports the poverty-level income for a family of four as a percentage of the median income for the same family type:

Figure 4

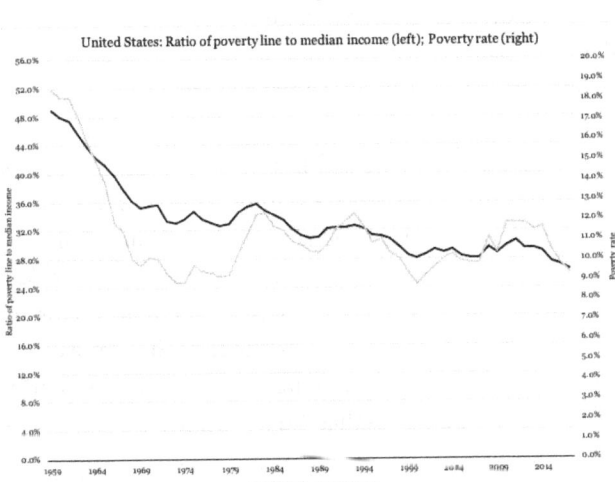

Source of raw data: *Census Bureau.*

Median income is for a four-person family; since the Census Bureau does not report poverty rates specifically for four-person families, the total poverty rate is used as a proxy.

7. Under an absolute definition, theoretically prices do not matter. According to the theory behind subsistence living in the iron law of wages, what matters is instead the basket of goods a person has access to. In practice, though, prices would matter with reference to the operating cost of providing the very basic benefits that an absolute-poverty welfare program would provide. What would not change over time, though, is the quality of the products involved; for example, the definition of a shelter would remain unchanged over time, even as the average house becomes bigger and more comfortable.

Prior to 1969, the poverty-to-median income ratio falls steadily. This reflects an absolute definition of poverty where there is no tie to the progress in overall household earnings. After the introduction of the relative poverty concept in 1964—going into effect with the 1965 fiscal year—and its update in 1969, the poverty-to-median income ratio essentially flattens out.

A similar pattern is visible in the poverty rate. Since the poverty rate stopped dropping, and since eligibility for welfare programs such as food stamps, Medicaid, cash assistance and public housing was tied to the poverty rate, demand for those programs was now guaranteed to be perennial. Even as economic growth—which was considerably higher in the 1960s through the 1990s than it has been so far in the 21st century—elevated the standard of living of all Americans, there was not a permanent, active role for the federal government to play in the economy. Until, that is, its role was changed, from provider of basic economic security to an agent of income redistribution.

The ideological intention behind this change is understandable against the background of Marxist economic theory. When the economic evolution of the Western world in general, and the United States in particular, disproved the hypothesis of perpetual suppression of workers' wages, the relative poverty concept made it possible for egalitarians to redefine the world in the image of their economic theory. Since poverty no longer declined, the world now looked as though it met the predictions that Marx had made about a capitalist class that did its best to keep workers in poverty so as to suppress wages.

Even more conspicuous is the policy implication of the relative definition of poverty. Only a complete redistribution of income, to the point where literally everyone makes the same amount, would guarantee the elimination of poverty. If this state of absolute egalitarianism were reached while plunging an entire nation into what is objectively a state of rampant poverty, it would not qualify as such by the relative poverty definition.

From an egalitarian standpoint, the redefinition of poverty has worked as intended. When the official measurement of poverty automatically increases the poverty threshold, the population eligible for help from the welfare state expands accordingly.

In Europe, the system of relative poverty is even more elaborate than in the United States. Eurostat, the statistics agency of the European Union, does not use a strict poverty concept, but refers instead to people "at risk of poverty". This is a broader concept than poverty itself, opening welfare-state programs for more people than just the poor.

A third segment, in addition to those who are poor and "at risk" of poverty, allows for yet broader expansion of welfare-state benefits. This segment consists of people who are "at risk of social exclusion". People in this category are not poor but cannot afford such things as a car or going on vacation.[8] Predictably, there is radical growth in the population eligible for entitlements under economic redistribution. For example, in a report from 2015 by the British Office of National Statistics, the three categories "poor", "at risk of poverty" and "at risk of social exclusion" covered 36 percent of the population. The official British poverty rate was less than half at 16 percent.[9]

There is another statistical tool to expand the entitled population. It is known as the "living wage". In a paper from 1999 for the U.S. Department of Labor's Division of Economic Research, Robert Shelburne with the United Nations explained the history of the concept and how it relates to the poverty definition:

> The living wage is a term used to define a "fair and decent" level of income that would enable workers to meet their "basic needs." There is no agreed upon definition of what specifically "basic needs" are nor is there an agreed upon methodology to determine basic needs; however, it is generally agreed that "basic needs" means more than mere physical subsistence and includes social needs that would allow a household a comfortable and decent standard of living.

He exemplifies what people "should" have access to under the living wage: "a nutritious diet, safe drinking water, suitable housing, energy, transportation, clothing, health care, child care, education, savings for long term purchases and emergencies, and some discretionary income". This concept is being advanced by egalitarians as the next frontier in economic redistribution. A group called Living Wage Action Coalition, founded in 2005, has developed a nationwide campaign for "fair wages" for employees on college campuses.[10] While the group's immediate focus is on "solidarity" between

---

8. Eurostat, the statistics agency of the European Union, provides a detailed definition. See: http://ec.europa.eu/eurostat/, AROPE database.

9. See: *Persistent Poverty in the UK and the EU: 2008-2013*, Office of National Statistics. Available at: ons.gov.uk.

10. See: livingwageaction.org.

students and workers, their ambitions reach far beyond campus borders. Adding specificity to to the definition provided in the U.S. Department of Labor report, the Living Wage Action Coalition explains that a living wage is "a decent wage" and "a complete consideration of the cost of living".[11]

While this definition is provided by an activist group and therefore may or may not be relevant to actual policy changes in the United States, it conveys the ideological principle underpinning the practice of egalitarianism and Marxist economic theory:

- Egalitarian ideology (formulated, e.g., in Rawls's *Theory of Justice*) prescribes that differences in liberty are mere reflections of differences in material possessions; both differences are considered inherently unjust;

- Marxist theory (as applied by, e.g., John Kenneth Galbraith) says that workers live at a lower standard of living because they are being deprived, by capitalists, of the alleged full value of their work.

By explaining income distribution between workers and capitalists as a power struggle, Marxist theory informs the egalitarian suggestion that there are no moral reasons why one man should live a wealthier life than another. This combination leads to policy initiatives and legislation. When government defines poverty as a standard of living lower than but essentially in constant relation to the median standard of living, it

- applies the moral argument from egalitarianism by making a person eligible for tax-paid entitlements based on his relative standard of living, not subsistence living; and

- incorporates the economic argument from Marxism by funding entitlements almost entirely by people with higher incomes.

Plainly: the relative definition of poverty perpetuates the need for the welfare state and guarantees that the pursuit of social justice will not end until every meaningful economic difference between individual citizens has been eradicated.

---

11. See: http://www.livingwageaction.org/resources_lw.htm#1

Marxism and social justice in the federal budget

From eminent domain to the definition of poverty, the egalitarian ideology has made major inroads into American society. For the better part of the past 100 years, government has been moving out of its minimal-state confinements and toward an extra-constitutional role in society and our economy. Initially, it was a matter of providing pensions for veterans, and special health insurance programs for very select groups. Prior to the Franklin Roosevelt administration, government incursions into economic redistribution were scarce and consequences for liberty were ideologically unintentional.

Under President Roosevelt, the federal government started operating limited welfare programs in a systematic fashion. They were still of a quality that made them fit in under a compassionately conservative headline, not leading to any intentional expansion of social justice. The goal was, namely, not to redistribute income among citizens, but to provide a tax-funded safety net as a last resort for people temporarily out of other options to provide for themselves. As mentioned earlier:

- In 1934 Congress created the National Housing Act, under which the U.S. government would provide a housing safety net for the poor and those with little income.

- In 1935, the Social Security Act established Aid to Dependent Children, a permanent unemployment insurance program and Social Security.

- In 1939 the food stamp program was born.

Despite the systematic approach, which is indicative of an early form of a welfare state, the ideological design of these programs is not egalitarian: the goal was not to fundamentally alter the outcomes of work, entrepreneurship and investment. As a result, there were only limited consequences for the character of the American constitutional republic:

Figure 5

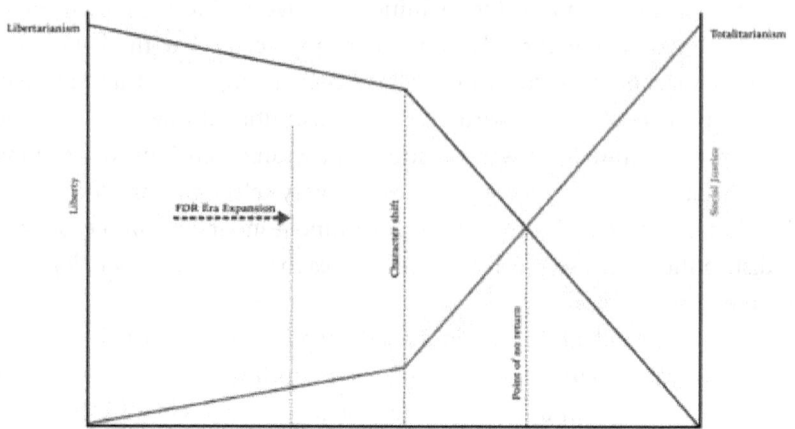

Despite the limited role of government in a pre-egalitarian welfare state, it still had negative repercussions for economic activity and prolonged the Great Depression.[12] One reason was the distinctly progressive profile of the federal personal income tax code. With the passage of the Sixteenth Amendment, Congress demoted income from its previous status of constitutionally protected property to a conditional state of ownership. If government deemed it could use the money better, then government would obtain it by raising taxes.

That is also what government did. As mentioned, this new taxation power meant that Congress could allow itself the discretion to use that tax for new government functions. Gradually, those new functions took on the same redistributive profile as the income tax had. However, the upmarch of egalitarianism through the federal budget came from the taxation side: already in its first three years with income-tax powers, from 1913 to 1916, Congress expanded the tax from seven brackets spanning tax rates between one and seven percent, to 14 brackets from two to fifteen percent.[13]

In order to fund the war efforts of World War I, Congress added another 42 brackets and topped out with a 77-percent tax rate on the highest incomes. While this expansion was ideological in nature—making higher-income earners do the heavy lifting in funding the military—the purpose

12. For a quality summary of this phenomenon, see Higgs (1995).

13. The data on personal income taxes is retrieved from an overview of the federal income tax, courtesy of the Tax Foundation's centennial commemoration of the 16th Amendment. See taxfoundation.org.

of the spending was temporary and, needless to say, not motivated by any egalitarian ambitions. Indeed, during the 1920s Congress rolled back its complexity, concluding with 23 brackets with rates up to 25 percent in 1925.

With the Great Depression, however, Congress reverted back to its ideologically driven quest for more tax revenue from higher incomes. In 1932 taxes once again rose sharply, with 55 tax brackets spanning from four to 63 percent. Despite reductions in the number of brackets during the 1930s, the top rate climbed to 79 percent. This shift was the first deliberate attempt to profile the personal income tax code based on a desire for economic redistribution. It also marked the explicit codification of the notion that personal income could be taken by government for an ideological goal. Privately earned property—income—was subject to the public purpose of funding redistributive government spending.

A war-funding peak during World War II put the bottom rate at 23 percent with a top rate at 94, with the span stabilizing between 20 and 91 percent in the 1950s. Then came President Kennedy, who signed the first growth-oriented American tax reform. It was a modest reform: the rates fell to 14-70 percent across 25 brackets. Alas, his reform did not mark any shift back to more traditional fiscal policy but perpetuated the idea that tax policy serves an egalitarian public purpose.

It was at this time that the spending side of the federal budget ideologically caught up with the tax code. Already prior to the War on Poverty and the birth of the egalitarian welfare state, the aforementioned welfare programs created an expansion route for entitlement programs. More importantly, Social Security claimed a rapidly growing share of total federal spending. As a telling image of the ideological transformation of the federal government, the budget share of minimal-state functions—national defense, law enforcement and infrastructure—accounted for 78 cents of every dollar Congress spent in 1954. In 1964 that share had fallen to 56 percent. Another ten years later, the minimal state claimed only 39 percent, with half the federal budget now being devoted to economic redistribution:

Figure 6

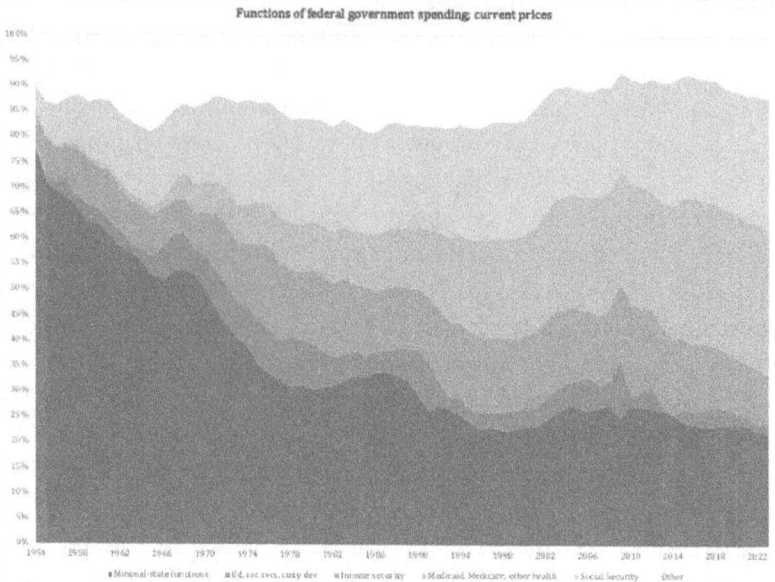

Source: *Office of Management and Budget*

In the late 1970s, the personal income tax became a central political issue as high inflation drove middle-class taxpayers into heavily burdensome tax brackets. Congress began responding during the Carter administration, but a major tax reform did not happen until under President Reagan. On his watch the number of tax brackets dropped from 16 to two, with the top rate declining radically, from 70 percent to 28 percent. While the bottom rate actually increased from zero (for a very narrow band of income) to 15 percent, deductions, a low top rate and overall simplicity restored a sense of property right to personal income.[14]

It is important to note, though, that the Reagan-era tax reform was an event isolated to the revenue side of government. It was not coupled with any reforms to rein in spending; the growth-oriented profile of the tax instead served the purpose of rapidly increasing revenue to fund the egalitarian welfare state. As a result, the egalitarian progress through the legislative branch, having built a substantial system of economic redistribution,

---

14. Since the Earned Income Tax Credit was enacted in 1975, it has effectively nullified federal income taxes on the lowest incomes.

remained largely unfettered by the Reagan presidency. There was never any challenge to the decades of work by Congress that had established a public purpose with government spending.

9

Restoring American Liberty

WITH THE END OF religious discrimination and slavery, and with the enactment of universal suffrage, America reached a point where, from an ideological viewpoint, she was a more perfect union. She still had many challenges to deal with, primarily government-enforced racial segregation in some states. Thanks in good part to courageous activists in the civil rights movement, the American constitutional republic was able to further expand liberty and the principle of equal opportunity.[1]

Yet while the American republic continued to expand individual freedom, she also began retreating in terms of economic freedom. While government stepped back from invading individual life based on a person's race, it stepped up its invasion of economic life. There is an ideological paradox in this, with libertarian ideals advancing in one area of American life while retreating in another.

How did this become possible? The explanation lies in the secularization of American life. When God is not the arbiter between liberty and social justice, the value of individual human life is no longer the prime criterion for government policy. Deliberations over policy are reduced to utilitarian considerations of whether or not a given piece of legislation, a given reform policy, will yield more or less of a given value. The nature of that value, in turn, is determined by government, as is its relation to individual citizens.

---

1. Tanner (2018).

All government involvement in the lives of individual citizens that goes beyond the protection of private life is driven by a desire to change outcomes of individual actions. To do so, government must forcefully redistribute economic resources, taking from some and giving to others. A good example, as we saw earlier, is from health care, where this rearrangement of outcomes between citizens can have highly tangible effects. When all medical services are provided through government, the best-practice method for allocating health care becomes a utilitarian exercise of calculations of costs and benefits of treatment.

So long as such calculations take place on an individual basis, between the patient and the doctor, it is a perfectly reasonable approach to best-evidence practice of medicine. However, there is no need for government to involve itself in that relation; what matters to a government that is interested in more than the protection of life, liberty and property, is to make cost-benefit calculations of the distribution of health care between individuals.

In order to redistribute health care, or any other resource, government needs to take jurisdiction not only over the resource itself, but the experience from that resource. This leads to increasingly invasive violations of the integrity of individual citizens.

Utilitarianism and the public purpose

In the philosophical literature, utilitarianism takes many forms, but they all have one character trait in common: the use of economic resources is given a moral value depending on the greatest perceived return on the use. While this seems reasonable at first glance, it is very different from the value theory of natural rights that underpins the U.S. Constitution.

In order to determine the greatest value of the use of a product, government prescribes a utilitarian value scale where the utility of a product is broken down into units, or "utils". These units can then be compared interpersonally, especially in terms of distributing government services. Suppose, e.g., that government runs a hunger relief program and has ten sandwiches available (we assume that it is pointless to give anyone half a sandwich). There are 50 people in line waiting for a sandwich.

How should government decide whom to feed and whom to leave hungry? A utilitarian method for allocating the food would dictate that the ten people who experience the greatest number of utils from being fed, should receive the sandwiches. The question is: who shall determine the utility that each person experiences?

If the individuals waiting to be fed are allowed to determine their own utility, every one of them will likely claim the maximum amount of utility and demand to be put first in line. Since there are more people in line than there are sandwiches, and since government has assumed the responsibility for distribution, it also has to decide on a distribution method that selects eligible individuals—and does so independently of what those individuals themselves believe that a sandwich is worth to them. Bluntly, the agency that runs the hunger program decides how to rank the individuals, regardless of what the individuals themselves may think.

In the *Kelo* case, the Supreme Court decided that the city of New London could use a similar principle to determine who should own property in the Fort Trumbull neighborhood. The city did not use "utils" as its scale to measure the best use of the land, but relied instead on expected tax revenue: the owners that resided in the neighborhood at the time the city designed its economic development plan were deemed by the NLDC to not be able to produce enough tax revenue. Other property owners would yield more tax revenue for the city.

Government decided that other individuals—other property owners—would be of higher value.

In the hunger program example, government decides that society is better off if it feeds one group of individuals as opposed to any other group. The ten people selected from the line of the hungry are deemed to have properties that, according to government, are better suited for the expense of nutrition, than any other selection of those in line. For example, government can use a criterion of workforce participation: the ten who get fed are more likely to be able to get a job and therefore pay taxes in the future.

In *Kelo*, the choice of property owners favors those who, according to government, are better suited to provide the tax revenue that government needs. Government selects a group of winners, using criteria that are independent of the will and desires of the individual citizen.

The use of utilitarianism to guide government policy—public policy—is fundamentally antithetical to the values upon which the U.S. Constitution was built. Its application to any right guaranteed by the Constitution collapses that right into a conditional proviso:

- Under natural rights, the value theory underpinning the Constitution, the individual is guaranteed a right unconditionally;

- Under a utilitarian value theory, the individual is guaranteed a right unless a higher value applies.

It is telling that, in the *Kelo* case, the Supreme Court gave local government a yardstick to determine its own success. This move by the Court was long in the making, as demonstrated by the *Midkiff* case from Hawaii. The ideological message in this allocation of the yardstick is even more apparent in the welfare state, where the success in terms of value is inherent to the amount of tax revenue coming in at one end of the government budget, and in the spending going out at the other end.

In fact, from a principled viewpoint the *Kelo* case merges with the welfare state at the point of taxation; in *Kelo*, expected tax revenue was the only measurement method that government used to gauge its economic-development success. Alas, effectively the utilitarian value was translated into tax revenue.[2]

The consequences of giving government a utilitarian yardstick go beyond the demotion of rights to conditional status. It embeds in the very institutions of government the ideological notion that government does not have to limit itself to being a Judge, but can in fact be a King. Utilitarianism allows, even makes necessary, this elevation of government: once the notion is established that it is morally right for a third party to question the allocation of resources through voluntary exchange, it is also established that the third party can use an independent quantitative method for that purpose. Once the evaluation is complete, it follows that whatever conclusion this third party draws is morally justified and implies a policy response.

Pointedly: once we grant moral approval to government to redistribute income and wealth, we give moral approval to the use of utilitarianism as a method for deciding how much to take from Jack to give to Joe. In doing

---

2. The Supreme Court notes a dissenting opinion in the *Kelo* case by three justices on the Connecticut State Supreme Court: (*Kelo*, p. 6):

> The three dissenting justices would have imposed a "heightened" standard of judicial review for takings justified by economic development. Although they agreed that the plan was intended to serve a valid public use, they would have found all the takings unconstitutional because the City had failed to adduce "clear and convincing evidence" that the economic benefits of the plan would in fact come to pass.

Despite the deterministic way in which the New London Development Corporation explained that property condemnation would lead to more tax revenue, the U.S. Supreme Court concluded that eminent domain "would be executed pursuant to a 'carefully considered' development plan".

so, we also give the evaluating party—the executive or legislative branch of government—the right to be the arbiter of its own actions.

Since economic redistribution means that government forcefully takes resources from private citizens, it also means that government puts itself in a situation of dispute. When the government that pursues redistribution also has jurisdiction over the decision whether it has failed or succeeded, there is no longer an independent arbiter involved. Government therefore can be as meticulous or as sloppy as it wants in setting up the criteria for its own success.

It is easy to see the consequences of this. In the War on Poverty, where the official goal was to eliminate poverty, government has clearly failed: the rate of poverty in the United States stopped declining when the War on Poverty started. Yet without an independent arbiter, the expansion of government that has taken place under the War on Poverty is not subject to any explicit evaluation.

In *Kelo*, the consequences are even more apparent of making government both arbiter and party to the case. The Supreme Court deferred the decision of success or failure in the pursuit of eminent domain to the city of New London. Hindsight has proven that the city of New London failed in its economic-development efforts: ten years after the case, the subdivision still sat largely empty.[3]

Furthermore, there is always the possibility that government will not be an independent arbiter when it is a part of the case. One of Robert Nozick's arguments for a minimal state is that parties in a disagreement tend to seek over-compensation when they want to exact justice; only an impartial judge can be trusted with solving the dispute.

The Court's decision to surrender the independent-arbiter function did not go unnoticed. In the words of dissenting Justice O'Connor:[4]

> We give considerable deference to legislature's determinations about what governmental activities will advantage the public. But were the political branches the sole arbiters of the public-private distinction, the Public Use Clause would amount to little more than hortatory fluff. And external, judicial check on how the public use requirement is interpreted, however limited, is necessary if this constraint on government power is to retain any meaning.

3. See: https://www.nationalreview.com/2015/06/kelo-eminent-domain-richard-epstein/

4. *Kelo v New London*, Dissenting opinion by Justice O'Connor, p. 5.

The solution would instead be utilitarian, with jurisdiction over the utilitarian yardstick being given to one of the parties in the dispute. To use Nozick's theory of the minimal state, this allows for the application of the moral code that defines the ultra-minimal state: protection against abuse of power depends on other criteria than respect for, and enforcement of, natural rights.

Beyond perverting the role of government, application of utilitarianism to government policy also violates Biblical theory of property. The Bible clearly uses natural-rights values in its explanation of property rights—a fact that should not be surprising, as we are endowed with natural rights by our Creator. These rights are absolute, and no other party may challenge them. This also means that there is no room for anyone to challenge them based on the proprietor's stewardship. In short: the proprietor retains jurisdiction over what it means to put his property to good use.

At the same time, property rights do not stand without moral obligation. God asks of every proprietor to exercise good stewardship. Economic resources are scarce by definition; idle wealth increases scarcity. Any person is free to accumulate as much resources as he can through voluntary exchange with others, but if he does not put that property to good use, he defies the moral imperative that God attaches to the property right. Matthew Chapter 25 explains this imperative with two examples (Matt. 25:2–10), the first of which is the story about ten virgins who went to meet a bridegroom:

> And five of them were wise, and five were foolish. They that were foolish took their lamps, and took no oil with them: But the wise took oil in their vessels with their lamps. While the bridegroom tarried, they all slumbered and slept. And at midnight there was a cry made, Behold, the bridegroom cometh; go ye out to meet him. Then all those virgins arose, and trimmed their lamps. And the foolish said unto the wise, Give us of your oil; for our lamps are gone out. But the wise answered, saying, Not so; lest there be not enough for us and you: but go ye rather to them that sell, and buy for yourselves. And while they went to buy, the bridegroom came; and they that were ready went in with him to the marriage: and the door was shut.

There are two layers to this story with reference to property. The first is that irresponsible stewardship squanders property: when it comes time to put it to good work, the owner is not ready. Those who would benefit from the proprietor's good stewardship will suffer as well.

Faith and Freedom

The second layer is the point about personal responsibility: if a proprietor fails to take good care of his property, nobody else has any obligation to help him. Furthermore, deliberate idleness or other forms of unproductive ownership is a violation of the moral imperative of good stewardship. Matthew highlights this with another example (25:14–18):[5]

> For the kingdom of heaven is as a man travelling into a far country, who called his own servants, and delivered unto them his goods. And unto one he gave five talents, to another two, and to another one; to every man according to his several ability; and straightway took his journey. Then he that had received the five talents went and traded with the same, and made them other five talents. And likewise he that had received two, he also gained other two. But he that had received one went and digged in the earth, and hid his lord's money.

When the lord of the servants returned, he praised and rewarded the stewardship that the first two servants had shown. The third servant, however, was punished for not having put his property to good use.

Matthew's examples explain that wasteful stewardship is immoral. There are two forms of wastefulness, one being that economic resources—in other words, resources that can satisfy needs and create prosperity—are always in scarcity. When property is not put to its proper use, scarcity increases unnecessarily.

The other form is the accumulation of wealth for the sake of accumulation, which is clearly distinguished from accumulation of wealth for productive purposes. For example, a man who becomes wealthy by engaging in gainful trade, provides something that others benefit from. By contrast, wealth as an instrument of beauty elevates wealth to where it is worshipped, thus competing with God. This is the point with the analogy of the camel and the eye of a needle (Mark 10:25): a wealthy man must be careful not to lose sight of the virtues of wealth. To simply own and accumulate is to corrupt the virtue of God's creation (Ps. 49:6–11).

However, the even more important message in the two examples from Matthew is that the morality in stewardship is never the matter of government. There is no window for an outside party to question how a proprietor uses his possessions. That is always a matter between him and God. Not even the term "blight" has any role to play in the matter of stewardship of property.

---

5. See also Ps. 112:5–9.

The absolute property right and the moral imperative of stewardship apply equally to all property owners, rich and poor alike. The man with five talents has the exact same responsibility to be a good steward of his resources as the man with two talents, or one. In reciprocity, they also have the same right to their property; the Biblical theory of property is directly applicable to the *Kelo* case, even though the property owners in general were not wealthy.

Specifically, there is no window in Biblical theory for government to question property rights. Again, not even the term "blight" can apply; if a man lets his property descend into disrepair, it is a moral matter between him and God. To give government blight-based authority to question property rights is to inject government into the moral relationship between God and man. Since the determination of blight always involves a utilitarian consideration of the state of the property, this also means that government would replace natural rights with utilitarianism as the value base of property rights.

Even if one accepts a window of blight as a reason for the forfeiture of property rights, legally conditioning that right on good stewardship, the application of utilitarianism is limited to exceptional circumstances. Specifically, when property owners responsibly take care of their property and put it to use as intended, what Justice O'Connor in her dissenting view refers to as "ordinary private use", there is no cause for eminent domain.

In fact, as if to emphasize the demarcation line between, on the one hand, a utilitarian challenge to property rights and, on the other hand, natural-rights based respect for property rights, blight was never an issue in *Kelo*. It was all about the unmitigated application of utilitarianism to property rights. Explained the Court:[6]

> There is no allegation that any of these properties is blighted or otherwise in poor condition; rather, they were condemned only because they happen to be located in the development area.

Christian Public Policy in Practice

The alternative to the welfare state is best understood as Christian public policy. The term is derived from the ethical principles discussed earlier,

---

6. *Kelo v New London*, Opinion, p. 4.

where the Bible informs not only private life but the relation between the state and the individual.

From the points made earlier about the Biblical principles for the state and the individual, follows a core principle that, if adhered to throughout society, will preserve and perpetuate a society under American liberty. That core principle is best summarized as responsible citizenship. It consists of three parts, all of which were discussed earlier:

a) <u>Work ethic</u>: each able man should work with his own hands (1 Thess. 4:11) and provide for those for whom he is responsible (1 Tim. 5:8-10, 6:8-10);

b) <u>Stewardship and charity</u>: treat charity not as an entitlement, but a moral duty (Ps. 112:5-9);

c) <u>Add value</u>: make private contributions to the social fabric of society (Lev. 19:15), take responsibility for your own children (Titus 2:1-8) and repay the community for what it provides for you (2 Thess. 3:7-10).

The purpose of responsible citizenship is to support the continued existence and steady improvement of a society where the individual is free to take advantage of opportunities, to pursue happiness and strive to make his own wishes and desires come true. To make this happen, individual citizens need to take responsibility for themselves and their families as well as their communities.

A society built on responsible citizenship is a society where American liberty is cared for, and passed on to future generations. It combines the values of Christianity with the ideology of libertarianism. However, the path to there from where America is today, is both long and demanding. It is a mistake to assume that there are any simple solutions—magic wands—that will bring our constitutional republic back in line with what our Founding Fathers intended. To do that will require endurance, commitment, selflessness and vigilance.

One of the most prolific misconceptions about libertarianism is that it means turning off the current welfare state like a light switch. This is an understandable misconception, as the idea is often purported by pop-culture libertarians and arrogant objectivists; to simply pull away government from its current commitments and activities in our economy would be to wreak havoc on tens of millions of Americans whose lives are now at the mercy of a government promise.

We simply cannot shut down welfare programs, Medicaid, Medicare, Social Security and other entitlement programs over night and hope for the best. The belief that this is possible springs from a wine-tasting level intellectual understanding of Adam Smith's concept of the invisible hand. Reforms that roll back the welfare state and replace it with freedom and opportunity must be carried out gradually and with unrelenting focus on those who are at the very bottom of our economic ladder.

The less a person has of his own making, the more he has become dependent on government; the more government takes away from that person in any given day, the harder he will fall. The harder he falls, the more difficult it will be for him to make good use of what a society of freedom and opportunity has to offer. In adjusting their lives to the welfare state, people have also made themselves unprepared for the immediate absence of the entitlements they enjoy. Whether that absence happens because of irresponsible libertarian reforms (an unlikely scenario) or through harsh fiscal necessities brought about by a debt crisis (far more likely) the effect on those dependent on government will be the same. They will be left out in the cold with no immediate way to replace the cash or in-kind entitlements that government provided them with.

Therefore, the one critical public-policy principle that springs from the exercise of responsible citizenship is that all reforms to restore American liberty must be designed to benefit the poorest Americans the most. The immediate duty of Christian public policy is to establish a path from today's welfare state and its social-justice driven economic redistribution, to an economy and a society of free, responsible and independent individuals, families and communities.

The following sections outline three examples of what it means to turn responsible citizenship into practice: a work-ethic reform for families to increase their self reliance; a reform to tap into stewardship and charity; and the meaning of adding individual value to a community.

When the Welfare State Fails

Aside the economic arguments against a redistributive welfare state, there is an argument to be made about moral consequences. These are consequences that proponents of the welfare state often overlook, especially in the United States where, so far, the deeply negative economic fallout of the welfare state has not yet materialized. Europe, on the other hand, is painfully familiar with those consequences, with Greece as the foremost, but far from only, example.

There is a considerable difficulty in discussing the moral side of the welfare state, especially among conservative American thinkers. The difficulty is in part associated with the formidable practical challenge in replacing the welfare state with private solutions to poverty relief and provision for those in need. Resistance to such solutions is understandable but not excusable: the monumental challenge in placing the first man on the moon did not deter President Kennedy from pursuing the goal.

Conservative resistance to systemic reform of the welfare state is instead to be found in a widely shared belief that it is better politically or economically—or both—to simply keep the welfare state and manage it with an adequate level of efficiency.[7] This notion is mistaken, here in America in the same sense as it has been in Europe where it has been widely shared among social democrats. Reforms in Scandinavian countries have allowed private providers of, e.g., health care and education under the banner of government funding and regulations. However, the result has only been a slowdown of the inevitable macroeconomic decay that always follows in the footsteps of the welfare state.

Eventually, the misunderstanding of "efficient" welfare-state management takes on fatal proportions: burdened by their welfare states, almost every economy in Europe has deteriorated into economic stagnation and industrial poverty.[8] That, in turn, has led to harsh fiscal measures directed at the very entitlement programs that are designed, funded and operated to provide for the poor and needy.

There is no better example of what a welfare state implosion looks like than that which happened in Greece. When the fiscal crisis broke out in 2008, the Greek government had already built a significant debt, the interest-rate costs on which increased substantially. At the same time, tax revenue plunged as unemployment rose and business investments contracted.

Pressured from a rapidly escalating debt crisis, the Greek government began rapid-fire cuts to its welfare state. From 2009 through 2014, cash benefits were cut by 13.5 percent while in-kind benefits were slashed by more than 45 percent.

---

7. In their book *Neoconservatism: An Obituary for an Idea*, C Bradley Thomson and Yaron Brook explain the neoconservative attitude toward the welfare state and how it came to influence the Republican party during the latter half of the 20th century.

8. Larson (2014, 2018b, 2018c).

Health care took a particularly hard hit. Spending on sickness benefits and health care dropped by 46 percent; examples by provider category:

Table 1. Spending Cuts in Greece

	Cuts
Dentists	-58.5%
Specialized hospitals	-43.2%
Ambulatory care	-41.3%
Retail medicine	-37.9%
General hospitals	-36.9%
Pharmacies	-36.3%
Medical, diagnostic laboratories	-26.8%
Ancillary svcs	-23.3%
Mental health facilities	-18.4%

Source: Eurostat

Another hard-hit entitlement was unemployment benefits. While unemployment tripled in 2009–2014, the Greek government reduced total spending on unemployment benefits from 3.4 billion euros to 1.9 billion euros. Per unemployed, the cut was almost unimaginable: from an annual 7,000 euros in 2009 to just over 1,500 euros in 2014. This is a 79-percent reduction, in current prices.

Housing benefits were almost eliminated, falling by 99 percent.

During the same period of time, taxes increased dramatically, from 39 percent of GDP to 50 percent. In 2015 the national value-added tax (VAT), which applies to both goods and services, increased from 13 to 23 percent.[9] It was the fifth increase since the beginning of the crisis and was followed by yet another increase in 2016.[10] A range of special taxes on imported products added to the cost of living.[11] In 2017 the same taxes increased again, topped off by a gasoline-tax increase.[12]

9. See: https://www.cnbc.com/2015/07/20/how-greek-firms-are-coping-with-massive-tax-hikes.html accessed 9/27/17

10. See: http://uk.reuters.com/article/uk-greece-economy-tax/greeces-vat-tax-hike-is-counterproductive-trade-association-idUKKCN0YF1DN accessed 9/27/17

11. See: https://www.theguardian.com/world/2016/may/16/tax-hikes-greece-coffee-austerity-economy-bailout accessed 9/27/17

12. See: http://www.dw.com/en/higher-tax-burden-for-greeks-in-2017/a-36974136 accessed 9/27/17

Personal income taxes increased substantially. The top rate of 40 percent expanded downward through the income layers, from an annual income of 70,000 euros in 2009 to 35,000 euros in 2012.[13] The top tax rate then increased in two steps, to reach 45 percent by 2016.[14]

These are just some examples of the tax increases that, in combination with heavy cuts in government spending, caused the Greek economy to contract by 25 percent during the fiscal crisis. For comparison, a similar loss of economic activity in the United States would take $5 trillion out of our GDP. It would cause some 40 million jobs to vanish.

Conventional wisdom would suggest that a crisis of this magnitude in the U.S. economy is unthinkable. It is important to remember that the same conventional-wisdom judgment applied to the Greek economy in the years prior to their fiscal crisis. In fact, when the European Union was formed and most of its member states joined the euro, many an economics expert stated that this new institutional structure would protect the Continent from fiscal crises in general.

Before the latest round of crises in European welfare states, several countries experienced serious downturns in the early 1990s. Sweden was perhaps hit the hardest.[15] Again, the economics expertise did not see the crisis coming; the concept of a crisis that increased unemployment from two to 15 percent in 18 months, crashed the currency and drove the Central Bank interest rate to 500 percent, was unthinkable.

The common denominator of crises in modern European countries is that they have all suffered from slow but gradually entrenching economic stagnation. Youth unemployment has increased gradually, household earnings have plateaued and, as a result, government has seen a slowdown in the growth of tax revenue. At the same time, eligibility for government entitlements has not relented—on the contrary, due precisely to the onset of economic stagnation, more people have become eligible and remained eligible for a longer period of time.

Welfare-state promises have become costlier, in absolute terms as entitlements cost more, and in relative terms as government outlays have grown faster than the ability of the taxpayers in the private sector to keep up. Inevitably, a rift opens in the macroeconomy, be it a sharp decline in exports for a small country with a large exports industry, or the bursting

---

13. On average at the time, one euro was worth $1.20–1.25.
14. http://www.bbc.com/news/world-europe-20996508 accessed 9/27/17
15. Larson (2014, ch. 2).

of a real-estate bubble, or any other significant event. When this "trigger event" happens, the path is short from the beginning of the downturn to a catastrophic hole in government finances.

Government quickly has to make a choice: try to save the economy from imploding or try to balance the budget. So far, the United States has avoided the escalation of a serious economic downturn into a full-blown, Greek-style fiscal crisis. The reason is in the combination of a somewhat limited welfare state and a central bank—the Federal Reserve—that has been able to provide the federal government with seemingly endless lines of credit with no serious harm to the U.S. Dollar.

There comes a point, however, when there is no padding left. If Congress completes the edifice of the welfare state, adding single-payer health care, single-payer universal child care and general income security (starting with paid family leave), the need for higher taxes is going to be acute. Then, in the next crisis, federal government spending is so high that no credit line from the Federal Reserve will be able to cover a rampant budget deficit. Taxes will already be so high that drastic tax increases will do major harm and aggravate the crisis.

This is the point where Congress would be at the mercy of foreign lenders in order to borrow to cover its deficit. Yet since the United States will be in an unprecedented situation with no domestic resources to finance its deficit, those lenders will demand an unprecedented risk premium in order to lend. Congress will be faced with the choice between paying crippling interest rates many times higher than in the last crisis—or make harsh, drastic, immediate Greek-style spending cuts. .

It is morally very irresponsible to place tens of millions of Americans on the receiving end of such spending cuts. When those cuts happen, namely, there will be no alternatives available for those who have become dependent on government. The spending cuts will not come with any reforms to open up private alternatives; institutionally, the programs that people depend on will remain in place. The only thing that changes is how Congress takes a chainsaw to the benefits.

In other words, there is no moral alternative to reforms that resurrect American liberty in its fullness. Those reforms aim to replace the current welfare state with solutions that are based on the principles of Christian public policy.

Work ethic: providing for our families

A central element of the principle that each man, to the best of his ability, should work with his own hands, is that he also provides for his family. We do not have more children than we can care for; we put no limit on our efforts to provide for the children we have. From a practical viewpoint, this means building financial security, such as for unplanned expenses or for longer-term, planned outlays.

Today, in America, it is difficult for many families to accomplish this. Far too many people live paycheck-to-paycheck lives, where the margins for financial uncertainties are negligible. While some of this is attributable to over-stretching in terms of material possessions, more often than not the reason is simply that the cost of living has been jacked up by taxes, fees and charges from government. Multiple layers of taxation compound the costliness of our daily lives: corporate income taxes diminish the margins for employers to compensate their employees; personal income taxes reduce take-home paychecks; sales taxes, use taxes and excise taxes elevate the cost of living; property taxes eat in to the housing budget.

Undoubtedly, families do get some return on their money, from public schools to infrastructure and protective services. They also get access to a welfare system if adverse life events happen. However, in addition to the question whether government is the best provider of those services, there is also the problem with an overly bureaucratized government and a tax-paid workforce dedicated to writing and enforcing regulations. This is the case with the federal government, whose employees are paid to—among countless examples—prevent farmers from collecting rain water, ensure that car manufacturers install backup cameras on their vehicles and enforcing license requirements for llama ranchers.

The regulatory burden of government also adds significant cost to the operation of businesses, even to the daily lives of America's families. How many thousands of dollars have car prices gone up because of regulations in the past 20, or even ten years? In other words, a reduction in the size of government red tape is a way to make it easier for more families to provide for themselves without having to live on the dole. However, instead of lining up behind the idea of a leaner, more affordable government, there is growing consensus among America's political leadership that government should instead expand its presence in the domain of family financial security.

Europeans know government programs for financial security as "paid leave": government compensates people who take time off from work by sending them a check for a share of their salary or wage. For example, when the mother of a newborn baby decides to stay home with her infant for some time after birth, a government agency replaces her work-based earnings for a certain number of months.

Other reasons for paid leave are for personal illness or to care for a sick child or another family member with medical conditions.

Support for paid-leave programs is growing in America, including legislation at the state level. As of December 2018, four states offer paid family leave to parents of newborns: California, New Jersey, New York and Rhode Island. The District of Columbia also has a program in place, and the state of Washington will start paying out benefits in January 2020.[16] Under Governor Jared Polis, Colorado is likely going to pursue its own paid-leave program.

In Congress, it is not just the Democrats who push for paid leave. Senator Rubio (R-FL) has turned a proposal from the conservative Independent Women's Forum (IWF) into the Economic Security for New Parents Act.[17] Given President Trump's support for the idea, as expressed in his first budget, there is a fair chance he would sign a bill if Congress sent him one.

The surge in support for paid leave has emerged despite the absence of studies on how much it would cost taxpayers. This is noteworthy; modeled after European standards, a full-scale federal paid-leave program could cost taxpayers close to $500 billion per year.[18] Bluntly: paid leave could overtake Medicare as one of the costliest entitlement programs in the federal budget.

It is also interesting to note the absence of any ideological debate over paid leave: with the build-up of conservative support, the conversation about government's role in the lives of American families has faded into the background. Some proponents of paid leave want it for ideological reasons; the non-economic motives of conservatives are more obscure.

There is, however, an alternative to paid leave that would satisfy ideological opponents and settle the issue for the foreseeable future. An overview of the paid-leave idea itself will set the case for the alternative.

---

16. See: http://www.ncsl.org/research/labor-and-employment/paid-family-leave-resources.aspx and http://lawfilesext.leg.wa.gov/biennium/2017-18/Pdf/Bills/Senate PassedLegislature/5975-S.PL.pdf

17. See: https://thinkprogress.org/pseudofeminst-group-marco-rubio-paid-leave-5f27056f65d1/ and https://www.congress.gov/bill/115th-congress/senate-bill/3345

18. See: https://papers.ssrn.com/sol3/papers.cfm?abstract_id=3015990

Paid family leave: an overview

The formal term for entitlement programs like paid family leave is "general income security". They resemble Social Security in that they provide income-style entitlements, but they differ in that the entitled population is of working age. In addition to paid family leave, general income security programs—as they exist in Europe—include paid sick leave, paid leave for parents to stay home with sick children and for the care of other family members. There have even been experiments with general leave time for unspecified personal reasons.

Benefits are based on a person's income, with replacement rates varying greatly. Existing European programs gravitate toward the 70–80 percent bracket; state-run programs in the United States offer lower replacements rates. They also replace income for a shorter period of time; while 6–12 weeks is the target in the United States, Canadian parents can take up to a year off, courtesy of taxpayers.

Funding normally comes from a payroll tax, which, combined with income-base benefits, theoretically means that every taxpayer is supposed to fund his own benefits. In practice, this model has proven difficult to maintain from a fiscal viewpoint, as exhibited by the very high payroll taxes in the Scandinavian countries. A similar model, used in Social Security, is expected to bankrupt the program in 2034.[19]

From an ideological viewpoint, there are clear similarities between Social Security and paid leave programs as we currently know them. They are all egalitarian, i.e., designed for economic redistribution. In Social Security, there is no direct relationship between a person's tax payments into a general income security program and his benefits withdrawal. Current tax revenue fund current benefits. All a taxpayer earns is a set of IOUs, claims on the system's future tax revenue. Technically, this means that Social Security redistributes money from the current working-age population to the elderly.

Furthermore, the benefits in Social Security are calculated based on a redistributive formula: the higher the income, the smaller the share that qualifies for benefits. By contrast, the Social Security tax is a flat rate of 6.2 percent up to a cap, currently $128,400. In other words, the funding of Social Security is slanted toward higher-income households, while

---

19. See: https://www.ssa.gov/oact/TR/2018/index.html

lower-income households benefit disproportionately as a larger share of their income counts toward their benefits.

Existing paid-leave programs in the United States are built with generally the same fiscal architecture. The paid family leave program in California, for example, caps weekly benefits at $435, which equals a pre-tax annual income of approximately $23,000.[20] By contrast, the payroll tax funding the program applies to incomes up to five times the average benefit ($118,371 in 2018). The estimated average annual wage in California for 2018 is $56,458, which means that the average taxpayer earns almost 2.5 times the maximum benefits. In other words, low-income workers benefit substantially more from the paid-leave program than higher-earning families. Furthermore, the payroll tax applies to all income earners, not just those having or planning to have children.

New York activated its paid-leave program this year. It has a similar profile, where the average benefit paid out, $652.95, is half the average wage on which the paid-leave payroll tax is levied.

At the national level, Senator Rubio's Economic Security for New Parents Act is based on Social Security and its redistributive architecture. The idea is, in fact, to allow parents to withdraw Social Security benefits already when they have children. There would be no new tax; current tax revenue is supposed to be sufficient.[21] Parents who use the paid-leave benefit would "repay" Social Security by delaying or diminishing benefits upon retirement.

A key problem with the Rubio-IWF program is that it is even more redistributive in nature than Social Security itself. In fact, Senator Rubio's own presentation of the proposal suggests that families earning up to $30,000 per year could cash in more than 100 percent of their annual income while on paid leave.[22] Those benefits would add to existing programs, such as the Earned Income Tax Credit, according to which a family

20. See: http://leginfo.legislature.ca.gov/faces/billTextClient.xhtml?bill_id=20152016 0AB908. This is calculated for a married couple filing jointly, ignoring all deductions. California paid-leave benefits are exempt from state income taxes but must be reported on the federal tax return.

21. This is a ruse. The period between the start-up of the program and the first repayments in the form of forfeited benefits would be several decades (assuming the mothers of newborns are typically 25–35 years of age), a period during which paid-leave benefits will create a substantial net drain of money from Social Security.

22. See: https://www.rubio.senate.gov/public/_cache/files/c434ed78-d855-4c7e-8716-4707d06f16b9/0E8DD4331CC02644842606DF4343990B.economic-security-for-new-parents-act-rubio-updated.pdf

with two income earners and two children and an annual income of up to $30,000 gets more from EITC than they pay in income taxes.[23] Given all other benefits the family can qualify for, they become a net taker as benefits exceed the personal income and Social Security taxes they pay.

Since federal income taxes are paid almost entirely by the upper half of all income earners, the Rubio-IWF program clearly belongs in the ideological camp that favors economic redistribution.[24] It reinforces the role of the federal government as an engine of economic redistribution and therefore raises the aforementioned moral question: is it right to place financially vulnerable families in critical dependency on a government that inevitably will default on its promises?

This is not a static question. Over time, tax-paid entitlements are prone to mission creep: the tend to grow in size and scope. General income security programs are bigger and more generous in other countries, suggesting that once a U.S. program is created, it will only change in one direction. This prediction is validated further by the fact that no federally funded entitlement program has ever shrunk, nor have they ever ended without being replaced by another.

Work ethic and financial security

In a perfectly libertarian world, every family, regardless of income, would be able to take care of its own financial security. However, since we do not live in a perfectly libertarian world, the better approach is to set eyes on reforms that can bring our country a good way down the road back to fully restored American liberty. One of the hallmarks of a good reform in this spirit is that it should promote and enable good work ethic.

In terms of financial security, the promotive element must consist of a realistic path for families of all incomes toward a reasonable balance in terms of disruption in work-based income. Building some financial security is helpful in elevating the experience of work from a mere chore to a sense of pride and achievement.

Financial security protects families against two forms of income disruption: the unexpected, such as unemployment or extended sick leave; and the planned, such as having a baby. Paid leave, as currently proposed in

---

23. Larson (2018, pp. 16–18).

24. See: https://www.stlouisfed.org/open-vault/2018/april/who-pays-income-taxes-how-much

the United States, addresses the latter. That is also a good starting point for reforms that give families the pride and independence to make major life decisions without having to take major financial risks.

One of the problems with government-run income security is that it severs the ties between a person's contributions to the system, in the form of tax payments, and the benefits he can collect. Like Social Security, the taxpayer earns "credits" for future collection of benefits based on his income; in reality, those credits are nothing more than IOUs issued by government. If there is not enough tax revenue available when we want to cash in those IOUs, we will not get any benefits. The impending bankruptcy of Social Security is a case in point.

An alternative reform, based on the principles of American liberty, would start with building a direct and unbreakable tie between a person's contributions toward his family's financial security, and his ability to withdraw money at some point in the future. Traditionally, this has been referred to as a "savings account" and is hardly dramatic enough to warrant any discussion. However, regular savings accounts suffer from a problematic drawback: deposits come out of our earnings after we have paid taxes on them.

Not considering income-based entitlements such as the Earned Income Tax Credit, the taxes even on lower incomes can be a problem for many families. When state income taxes are added, the chunk taken out of a paycheck becomes noticeable. For example, in eight states a married couple filing jointly, making $40,000 per year, will pay a marginal state income tax in excess of six percent. This comes on top of the federal income tax, which is ten percent on the first half of their income, then rises to 12 percent.

Therefore, a good reform allows people to use their pre-tax earnings in order to build financial security for the future. The reform creates an account—let us call it Family Freedom Account (FFA) for reference—into which workers can deposit portions of their paychecks, while deferring the payment of federal and state income taxes. Those taxes are paid when the owner of the FFA makes a withdrawal.

The FFA is individual (or jointly owned if so desired) which means that all deposits are the property of the account owner. Knowing that the money is always available is in itself a significant contribution toward financial security; another contributing factor is the proportionality between deposits and money available. Under tax-run income security programs, people who earn more money lose more money when using the government program than those who earn less. Furthermore, the benefit is determined by Congress or the state legislature (depending on whether the program is federal or state-run), allowing for no flexibility in a family's financial planning.

In addition, a tax-funded income security program requires its own tax, which is added to current taxes on personal income. This in turn reduces the margin that people have for their own savings. With the FFA, families are given the opportunity to increase deposits when they have margins in their own finances, and reduce them for tougher times. Likewise, they can withdraw a larger or smaller portion of their deposits, thereby allowing for shorter or longer leave in accordance with their circumstances at the time the money is needed. Furthermore, since the deposits are proportionate to income, the financial security offered by a family's FFA is proportionate to their living expenses; since we adjust our cost of living to our earnings, the individuality of the FFA allows for financial security even with small deposits.

The terms for withdrawal should be permissive, allowing families a great deal of discretion in how they use the money. However, since there is a tax-deferment component related to the accounts, it is highly unlikely that Congress would allow people to deposit money and defer taxes for any reason they wanted to. Therefore, it is realistic to expect certain restrictions on the use. (Narrowing down the reasons for withdrawal would also prevent that FFAs become a form of unemployment insurance; the purpose of the FFA is to allow for expectable events causing income losses.) Those reasons would be

- Leave to care for a newborn or a sick child that has to be home from school;
- Absence related to one's own, non-emergency medical conditions (again differentiating between expectable and non-expectable events), where the account would not pay for medical costs but exclusively replace lost income;
- Care for a relative, such as a spouse or an elderly parent.

Income taxes, deferred at deposit, would be paid upon withdrawal. Since the account holder would have full control over the withdrawals (under specified terms), he or she can choose to take less out of the account than the income lost. That way, the deposits can last longer than they would at dollar-for-dollar withdrawal and possibly, temporarily drop the income earner into a lower tax bracket.

To illustrate the mechanics of the Family Freedom Account (FFA), suppose a married couple, Jack and Jill, start working right out of college, at the age of 22. Jack makes $35,000 and Jill makes $28,000. They get raises that, over time, equal two percent per year, on average. Prices are assumed constant. They have a joint FFA where they deposit six percent of Jack's pre-tax income and four percent of Jill's pre-tax income. After their first child is born and their cost of living goes up, they reduce their savings rates to four and two percent, respectively.

For simplicity, suppose they only make withdrawals from the account to be home with a newborn baby. They have three children, the years they turn 28, 32 and 36.

We assume that Jill chooses to stay home, and that she withdraws funds from the FFA equal to 75 percent of her current income. If she stays at home for six months with each one of her children, their FFA is still going to have a reasonable balance: between their first child being born and their 40th birthdays, Jack and Jill will never have less than nine weeks' worth of income replacement (at 75 percent of Jill's income) in their FFA.

Figure 7 illustrates the hypothetical balance in their account:

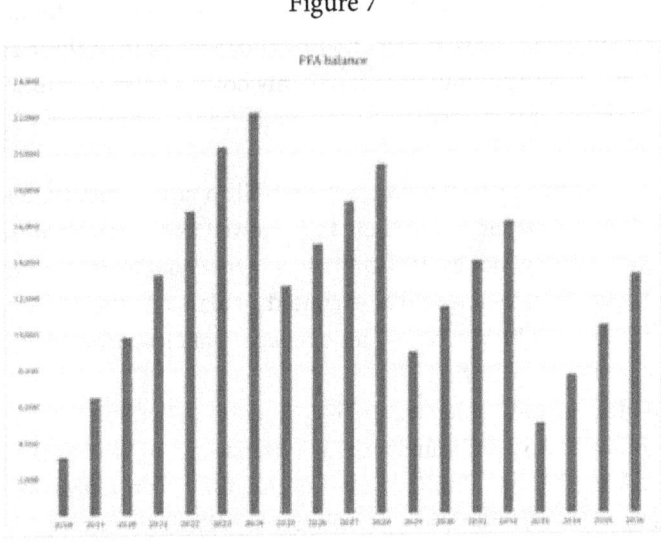

Figure 7

There are several assumptions behind this example that are up for debate. First of all, their combined federal, state and local income tax burden is assumed to be constant. Over a period of 18 years, it is likely that the burden would change at least a couple of times. Any such changes would raise a question as to what tax burden Jack and Jill should face on their FFA withdrawals: the tax burden at the time of deposit—at which point they deferred income taxes—or at the time of withdrawal.

To keep the system simple, it would be reasonable to assume that taxes are paid according to the rates at the time of withdrawal. Any other model would require complicated accrued-tax liability calculations, which would add unnecessary complexity to the FFA model.

A tax-at-withdrawal rule also discourages legislators from raising income taxes, as people will notice how such tax increases diminish their deposits.

Secondly, the example is based on an assumption that there are no legal hindrances or disincentives for people who take FFA-funded leave. For example, at the time their first child is born, Jill can finance 48 weeks of leave at 75 percent income replacement, and still not deplete their FFA entirely. It is implied that she can take 26 weeks off without any risk to her employment; in some government-run systems, such as in Sweden or Canada, a parent can be on paid leave for up to a year without risk of being laid off.

Third, it is assumed that Jack and Jill do not use their FFA for anything other than to finance leave for six months after each of their three children is born. Since at one point their account only holds a balance of nine weeks' worth of income, it is likely that they would be conservative with paid leave for any other reason.

It is, of course, possible for Jack and Jill to adjust the share of their income that they deposit onto their FFA, as well as the rate at which they choose to withdraw money. If withdrawals were equal to 65 percent of income instead of 75, they would always hold a balance in their FFA equal to at least 36 weeks of Jill's income. This opens for paid leave for other reasons than to care for a newborn.

An income replacement rate of 65 percent is in tandem with what tax-paid income security programs provide internationally. Since it is assumed in the FFA model that families would decide their own replacement rate, this number should be considered only as part of an experiment. However, it does illustrate that the FFA model has significant potential in helping families build financial security even under relatively modest conditions.

The FFA and government tax revenue

Since the FFA allows taxpayers to defer federal, state and local income taxes, it is a valid concern to ask how this will affect government tax revenue. A simple experiment indicates that there would be a minimal reduction in tax revenue collections, small enough to resemble an accounting error. At the same time, the calculations for the FFA tax revenue loss assumes that all government employees use their accounts, which ostensibly would reduce the cost of paid leave for governments. These savings are not included in the following estimates.

The two key variables to estimating the fiscal impact of FFAs are the deferred tax payments as people save out of pre-tax income, and the taxes paid on withdrawals for eligible paid leave. The first variable is found as follows.

Savings are assumed to come out of total personal income, which includes compensation of employees, proprietors' income, dividend and interest, and transfers from government.[25] The reasoning behind this is that people do not make a difference between source of income when they calculate their savings margins.

Withdrawals, on the other hand, are dimensioned to replace employee compensation (CoE). Since non-work income continues to roll in regardless of whether a person works or not, it is reasonable to measure withdrawals exclusively to match CoE.

Since CoE is approximately 63 percent of personal income, there is a potential for gradual build-up of balances in the FFA system. Such balances will primarily benefit middle-age workers, who can be expected to take more sick leave than younger workers. On the other hand, workers in the reproductive age 18–40 is the demographic that will use paid leave to care for newborns.

If we assume that people will put savings into their FFAs proportionate to what they expect to need—and not explicitly try to build large balances—it is reasonable to expect a savings rate of two percent of personal

---

25. It is worth noting that the transfers category is greater than "dividend and interest". This is yet another reason to take a skeptical look at proposals for paid family leave that include new tax-funded transfer payments to households.

income. Older workers can be assumed to save less, since they will not be using the FFAs for paid parental leave, with younger workers saving more for that very purpose.

On the withdrawal side, it is assumed that workers on average take out 60 percent of their employee compensation for sick leave and 65 percent to care for newborns. The 65-percent rate is assumed to apply to younger workers, whose margins between income and cost of living is smaller.

To calculate aggregated values for deferred taxes and taxes paid on withdrawn benefits, the following numbers are used:

- Personal income is $16 trillion
- Compensation of employees is 62.5 percent of personal income, or $10 trillion
- Total federal, state and local personal income taxes paid are 12.4 percent of personal income, or $1.98 trillion

These values are proxies for the first quarter of 2018. The three variables are assumed to grow in constant proportions to each other, with the growth rate of three percent being an extrapolation of recent Bureau of Economic Analysis data over personal income.

It is assumed that every employed worker takes two weeks of paid sick leave, on average, per year. On the parental side, it is assumed that every parent of a newborn takes, on average, three months paid leave. There are four million live births per year, with an assumption of a one-percent annual increase. In all, the withdrawals of paid-leave compensation from FFAs will amount to:

- $250.02 billion for sick leave, and
- $28.8 billion for the care of newborns, for a total of
- $278.82 billion.

in the first year calculated. Savings, again two percent of personal income, would amount to $320 billion.

Based on these figures, workers defer an estimated $39.7 billion in income taxes, while paying an estimated $34.6 billion on FFA withdrawals. This is a 12.9-percent tax cash-flow deficit, though that deficit is only 0.3 percent of total personal income taxes collected, or approximately 0.18 percent of all federal, state and local taxes collected.

These calculations are based on a stylized experiment and should therefore not be taken as a final verdict on how the FFA model would impact government budgets. However, it provides an analytical understanding of the mechanisms at work, and it does suggest that the FFA is of little consequence to government finances in general.

At the same time, it would make a significant difference in the lives of working families across America. It is not the cut that solves the Gordian knot, but it is a step forward for market-based financial independence. Furthermore, since the FFA provides a savings incentive toward private financial security, and does so without expanding government, it also increases the independence of America's families of a government budget that is increasingly vulnerable to a debt crisis.

Stewardship and charity: a reform idea

Christian public policy relies equally on the promotion of work ethic as it does on responsible stewardship of property. Since property includes wealth, this means that America's wealthy have a moral responsibility to not let their wealth lay idle.

This is not a cliché. As the Bible explains, idle wealth is detrimental to a nation's ability to build and sustain prosperity. There are, of course, good arguments from economics to the same effect, but even common sense suggests that if a man accumulates vast wealth and simply stashes it away somewhere, opportunities will be lost to others who could have made good use of that wealth for entrepreneurial projects.

Superficially, these points can be taken as an argument for high taxes on the wealthy. That is not the case. It is of paramount importance that any man who builds wealth is free to manage it as he sees fit; as soon as government is given a say in how a man should dispose of his wealth, we leave the realm of liberty and embark on another ideological path. In addition to the moral arguments against social justice outlined in this book, there are also important economic arguments against any government involvement in the stewardship of wealth. For one, there is no country in human history where government has put confiscatory limitations on wealth, that has also continued to thrive economically.

Quite the contrary: human history is rife with examples of government-run economies that have pulled countries into poverty and despair.

There is no need to regurgitate that evidence here; suffice it to say that private wealth is best managed by its rightful owners.

But how, then, are we to guarantee productive, responsible stewardship of that wealth? How do we know that when we speak of a moral responsibility for the wealthy to not idle their resources, we will not be preaching into the wind?

To begin with, it is important to humanize the wealthy. Like everyone else, they are individuals with aspirations, desires, compassion and moral preferences. They want to leave the world a bit better than they found it, and like all of us, they take pride in making a difference.

Furthermore, it is unproductive, not to say distractive, to distinguish between "wealthy" people and those who are "not wealthy". Wealth is a continuum, beginning with very small means and gradually expanding to include those who own tens, even hundreds of billions of dollars. Any discrimination of the "wealthy" is arbitrary and therefore useless for the consideration of their role in public policy.

Another important aspect of wealth is that very few who have a lot of it will ever let their possessions lay around. The old image of Scrooge McDuck and his bank vault filled with gold coins may make for a colorful caricature of the wealthy, but it is far from reality. Millionaires and billionaires invest their money in stocks, i.e., ownership of corporations, thus allowing those corporations to grow, thrive, create jobs and put out products that make a difference for the better in people's lives.

Wealthy people also donate generously to worthy causes. Hospitals, universities, research institutions and charitable organizations helping those in need, all benefit from the proceeds of wealth. In other words, to make a point about responsible stewardship of property is not to suggest wealthy people keep their wealth locked up somewhere.

The discussion of stewardship and charity is, instead, a discussion of how we as a country can tap into the desires of the wealthy to be productive citizens and make a difference in our communities. However, this ambition is not limited to the wealthy, but it includes all of us. However large or small wealth we have, we are all morally obligated—under American liberty—to use our resources in such a way that we make the best possible contribution to the future for ourselves, our loved ones and our communities.

Our shared desire to be good stewards of our private resources is an ambition that could be put to good work in advancing Christian public policy. When seen in combination with its twin virtue, charity, good stewardship forms a channel that can advance reform in an area that is of particular importance to the resurrection of American liberty.

That area is the caring for the poor, colloquially known as "welfare". It is part of the widespread problem we have created for ourselves, of making large numbers of Americans dependent on government to make ends meet every month. In addition to creating a reciprocated obligation on others to provide the resources, the entitlement programs upon which people depend trap millions of families in a situation where they are discouraged from providing for themselves, while being put at the increasingly dire risk of a government default on its promises.

Yet despite the pressing need for true welfare reform, little has been done in American politics to advance good reform ideas. In the meantime, the dependency on government handouts continues to increase. The expansion of the welfare state has significantly reduced work-based income as part of the finances of low-income families. In 1957, wages and salaries accounted for almost two thirds of average personal income; as of 2017, that share was down to 50 percent. At the same time, transfers—entitlements—increased from five percent in 1957 to 17 percent in 2017.

Welfare reform is a key to the restoration of self reliance; charity, in turn, is a key to welfare reform. Plainly: in order to scale back dependency on government, we need to tap into the charitable character of the American people.

There is a lot of potential in this: compared to the rest of the world, Americans continue to be impressively charitable.[26] Since charity is one of the most worthy forms of good stewardship, our common appreciation of this form of community involvement provides a good starting point for productive, liberty-oriented welfare reform.

In order to be successful in this regard, a reform to our welfare programs must have the goal of transferring responsibility for caring for the poor and needy from the federal government—where most of the funding and regulations are currently determined—down to local communities and individual citizens. A reform of this kind would be complex—but not complicated—and must be gradual in its progress. Specifically, it must open for individuals to participate with both their money and their moral preferences.

---

26. Brooks (2006).

Welfare reform done right

Private charities already do this today. The focus of a new welfare reform is not on charities that already operate with private contributions, but on bringing the principles of private charity into the realm of tax-paid welfare. To do so, a reform effort should:

1. Decentralize control to expand moral involvement—by traditional enumeration of powers, whatever jurisdictions over welfare programs that are not explicitly left with the federal government, belongs to the states or whomever they delegate it to;
2. Encourage monetary contributions—a dollar-for-dollar deduction is especially attractive for people of high net worth; for every $1 a person donates to a charity of his choice allows him to make a dollar-for-dollar deduction from his personal federal income taxes;
3. Latitude for experimentation—charitable organizations should be allowed to innovate within a minimum framework of regulations.

Decentralization is essential to involve communities of all kinds. It is also the one piece of reform that faces the greatest legislative challenge. Today, welfare programs in the United States are funded and regulated to a large degree by the federal government. Therefore, a first step toward bringing control over welfare programs back to local communities must be to reduce and eventually eliminate the role of the federal government. This is done by means of separating two key jurisdictional questions over welfare programs:

- What is the goal of the program?
- How is the goal to be accomplished?

Congress defines the goal of a welfare program, such as Temporary Assistance to Needy Families (TANF). Currently, the federal government also controls how states are to accomplish that goal, i.e., provide help to those in need: Title IV, Part A of the Social Security Act specifies the purpose of federal TANF grants to states as being to

- Provide assistance to needy families in order to secure that children can be cared for by their own families;
- End dependence on government benefits by promoting workforce participation and marriage;

- Prevent and reduce out-of-wedlock pregnancies, including quantitative goals for said reduction; and
- Encourage two-parent families.

Congress has stated these goals for TANF as tied to the grants that states receive for running the program. Decentralization therefore begins with giving states jurisdictions over how to attain the goals—and for states to gradually decentralize that jurisdiction further, all the way to local community groups, churches and others.

Today, the "how" question is answered by Section 404 in Title IV where, today, state use of the funds are restricted to fascinating detail. For example, the share that may go toward administrative costs is specified, without an accompanying definition of administration.

Even though Section 404 opens with language that is supposed to liberate states in how they use the TANF funds, Section 403 leads states by the hand down a narrow path of how to run TANF.[27] As often as it can,

27. The subsection that puts "limitation on use of funds for activities promoting responsible fatherhood" provides an excellent example (see Title IV, Section 403 of the Social Security Act): "(I) Activities to promote marriage or sustain marriage through activities such as counseling, mentoring, disseminating information about the benefits of marriage and 2-parent involvement for children, enhancing relationship skills, education regarding how to control aggressive behavior, disseminating information on the causes of domestic violence and child abuse, marriage preparation programs, premarital counseling, marital inventories, skills-based marriage education, financial planning seminars, including improving a family's ability to effectively manage family business affairs by means such as education, counseling, or mentoring on matters related to family finances, including household management, budgeting, banking, and handling of financial transactions and home maintenance, and divorce education and reduction programs, including mediation and counseling.(II) Activities to promote responsible parenting through activities such as counseling, mentoring, and mediation, disseminating information about good parenting practices, skills-based parenting education, encouraging child support payments, and other methods.(III) Activities to foster economic stability by helping fathers improve their economic status by providing activities such as work first services, job search, job training, subsidized employment, job retention, job enhancement, and encouraging education, including career-advancing education, dissemination of employment materials, coordination with existing employment services such as welfare-to-work programs, referrals to local employment training initiatives, and other methods.(IV) Activities to promote responsible fatherhood that are conducted through a contract with a nationally recognized, nonprofit fatherhood promotion organization, such as the development, promotion, and distribution of a media campaign to encourage the appropriate involvement of parents in the life of any child and specifically the issue of responsible fatherhood, and the development of a national clearinghouse to assist States and communities in efforts to promote and support marriage and responsible fatherhood."

Congress blurs, crosses and even eliminates the line between the questions "What is the goal of the program?" and "How is the goal to be accomplished?" That must change.

There was an attempt in 1996, when Congress passed PRWORA, a.k.a., welfare reform. This reform aimed to transform welfare, give states greater control over it and open for a more localized decision and implementation process over funds and aid. However, as the current examples demonstrate, that did not happen, and there is a particular reason for this. Programs such as TANF, SNAP (formerly known as food stamps) and the Earned Income Tax Credit (EITC) are not designed to provide poverty relief. They all serve a common ideological purpose, namely to redistribute income between citizens.

To this point, it is telling how poverty has remained stable in the United States over the past half century, despite substantial growth in GDP and household income. The reason, as mentioned earlier, is the statistical definition of poverty as used by the federal government, which changed with the beginning of the War on Poverty in 1964. Once poverty is defined as a de facto percentage of median income—as opposed to an absolute standard of living—the programs that dispense benefits based on poverty status do so in order to further the ideological goals of social justice. As evidence of their shift in purpose, the appendix to this chapter reports the official poverty rate for American families as percent of total population.

So long as the purpose of welfare programs is to redistribute income, not to alleviate poverty, Congress cannot give up anything more than limited control over the welfare programs. In other words, a decentralization reform would require that Congress gave up its commitment to social justice and allowed states to define their welfare programs based on the ideological preferences of their choice. States that want to continue the programs based on social justice and economic redistribution should be allowed to do so; states that prefer to return them to the purpose of poverty relief should feel free to do that.

Since decentralization requires Congress to resign authority over how welfare programs are run it must limit itself to answering the question "What is the goal of welfare programs?" During an intermediate period, the federal government also maintains its funding of those programs, hence the dollar-for-dollar tax deduction.

To accomplish this, Congress should authorize the states to create a Charity Compact, which rests on three principles:[28]

a) Private provision of help to those in need;

b) State jurisdiction over benefits and the terms of eligibility;

c) Dollar for dollar deduction from personal federal income taxes for donations to the Charity Compact.

The purpose of the compact is to function as a minimally invasive agency for federally sponsored welfare programs. Its role is to register and authorize private providers of welfare, to monitor compliance with the terms set by the state, and to audit the provision of welfare, including funding. The state, again, is free to choose to what degree it wants to impose regulations on charities participating in the compact. However, the more of a heavy-handed approach the state takes, the less likely it is to encourage community involvement.

Furthermore, since the Compact is limited to tax-funded welfare programs, a tight regulatory grip by the state is likely to drive the more innovative, active and passionate organizations into charity operations entirely outside of the tax-funded programs under the Compact. Therefore, true decentralization goes hand in hand with true deregulation.

In other words, the Compact replaces all existing state agencies involved in welfare programs. This should vouch for a sizable reduction in administrative costs, which are currently capped at a notably high 15 percent of program costs.

The participation of private providers is key to the decentralization of tax-funded welfare programs. To be eligible, a charity provider must obtain a certificate of approval from the Compact; the approval process is to guarantee that the funding—which consists of redirection of federal funds—is proper and minimizes the risk for tax fraud. However, the nature of the approval process must be minimalistic and focused on accountability to protect those who receive welfare and those who donate money. The point, namely, is to allow for a diverse set of providers with different philosophies, to give those in need a variety of options for help.

Inevitably, this means that there can be two organizations working side by side with different ideas on how to provide welfare. Suppose Hand-OutHere is driven by a desire to provide as much money as possible with

---

28. For the original study of the Charity Compact idea, see Larson (2012).

the most lenient restrictions, while HandToHelp puts tighter conditions on help, requiring welfare recipients to show progress toward self sufficiency. As a practical matter, this means that welfare recipients get to choose which organization to apply for help from; some will gravitate toward HandOutHere while others will seek help from HandToHelp.

An obvious concern here is that people on welfare would for the most part prefer the cash that is more easily obtained and therefore crowd to HandOutHere. It would be wrong to *a priori* assume that this is the case, but the concern is valid. After all, some of the criticism often presented toward the existing welfare system is that it discourages work and encourages sloth and indolence. Whether or not this is true is a matter for another discussion; what is clear, though, is that when welfare programs are supposed to help people under a *relative* definition of poverty, they are by definition redistributive and those eligible can stay eligible simply by virtue of making a certain percentage of median income.

However, the worries about promoting inactivity are addressed by the very construction of the Compact. The funding for welfare programs through the Compact comes from taxpayers, but they are not provided on the basis of traditional appropriations. They come from donations, where taxpayers write checks to the provider of preference; the donation is reciprocated with a dollar-for-dollar deduction of the donor's personal, federal income tax.

Taxpayers can choose the organization that provides the help they prefer to see for people in need. Those who prefer a lenient handout will donate to HandOutHere, while those who are more concerned with helping people to a better life will give their money to HandToHelp. In other words, moral preferences interact with the free market.

It is reasonable to expect that there will be a balance between the moral preferences of donors and the kind of help people will seek. Human nature is in general geared toward compassion in combination with the pride of self determination. This does not mean that only the stricter form of help will be provided; there will always be those who believe in economic redistribution to the point where they will gladly donate toward that purpose, even within the framework of a welfare charity. However, if—as some may suggest—most people in need of help prefer HandOutHere while most donors prefer HandToHelp, the former provider will run out of cash while the latter will have an abundance available. The prevailing moral preference of the donors will then win over those who really need help, as they come over to HandToHelp and accept their terms of welfare.

By the same token, if taxpayers in abundance prefer to support HandOutHere, their moral preferences will dominate the way people in need are being provided for. The point is to allow people to make individualized, informed moral choices, both as providers of help and as recipients.

Value through selflessness

To add value to a community is to put the needs of others above one's own. There are few ways that God gives us a chance to grow as significantly as when we are provided with an opportunity to be selfless. Yet there is no more crucial building block in human character and responsible citizenship than the willingness to provide for others without the expectation of personal reward.

In God's words, we shall avoid self-promotion and "study to be quiet". This imperative is to guide us in every aspect of our lives, from the daily deeds of parenting, work and charity to the Herculean moral task of laying down one's life to protect others.

Selflessness, again, is a cornerstone of a free society. At the edge—in a situation where liberty is faced with an existential threat—all men may be asked to make the ultimate sacrifice to secure the continued existence and future of a free, peaceful society. We hire some to do this job for us, whether in the armed forces or in law enforcement, but in time of crisis there is no dichotomy between men whose duty it is to protect, and those who are relieved of that duty. It has been said that in times of crisis, all private plans are repealed; whether this calls on able men to pick up arms or in other ways provide for the survival of their society is a question for the occasion. What matters is that liberty will not survive a challenge if some men see it as their entitlement to stay away from its protection.

When liberty is not threatened by a crisis, it still needs support by responsible citizenship. In addition to the ethical exercise of work and family life, and the active, charitable participation in our community, this means participating in functions that secure the continued existence of the foundations of our society, such as legislative and other public service. Since, in a society without a welfare state, the functions of government are strictly limited, there is no career to be had, let alone personal wealth to be built, from holding elected office. Public service is supposed to be selfless in the genuine sense of the word.

It is also needed of all able members of a community. If participation in legislative and other public affairs is left to the few, there is always a risk that marginal ideological preferences gain more influence than they warrant. For example, if 90 percent of all men and women in a community are libertarians, and ten percent favor social justice, and all libertarians consider public service a chore to be avoided, then the ten percent social-justice proponents may come to entirely dominate legislative and other elected offices. Even if most voters do not share those values, all it takes is that the only candidate is a promoter of social justice.

Selflessness thus means protecting and preserving liberty. To be able to exercise such selflessness, a man must let go of indulgences that elevate his own needs above those of the community. Among those indulgences are drugs, such as but not limited to alcohol and cannabis. In this context, the current debate over legalization of cannabis stands out as one of the defining moral issues of our time.

Proponents of legalization often claim to stand on a foundation of individual freedom, in other words, to be libertarians.[29] Viewed in narrow isolation, they are correct: it is certainly the case that in a free society, people should have the right to use whatever substances they want and take the consequences of their use - and abuse.

There are two lines of arguments against legalization, one pertaining to the violent behavior that follows consumption of some drugs. Some suggest, convincingly, that cannabis is a catalyst for psychotic and violent behavior. Let us accept their argument as valid and make clear that this is not an argument against cannabis per se, but a general point against the use of drugs that cause violent behavior. Cannabis becomes a pertinent example simply because of the legalization debate.[30]

Assuming that cannabis does indeed lead to psychotic, violent behavior in a large enough share of the population that use it, the question arises what effects this behavior has on the peace and liberty of the community where those individuals live.

---

29. The Libertarian Party, e.g., is unequivocally for legalization on the grounds of individual freedom. See: https://www.lp.org/issues/war-on-drugs/

30. In fact, one could make the case that our society has enough problems with alcohol as a cause of violence, that we do not need other drugs with similar, perhaps even worse effects in terms of destructive behavior.

Furthermore, an addiction impedes a person's ability to make rational, informed decisions: by definition, the addiction places higher emotional value on a person's own needs than his duties toward any other person. This may not lead him to make an egoistic choice at every turn, but on balance his acts and decisions are irrationally driven by his own needs. So long as irrational behavior is limited in a person's everyday life, it does not influence his ability to function as a fully adult member of society. The problem comes when irrational, addictive behavior degrades a person's ability to support himself and his loved ones and when he becomes more interested in satisfying his addiction than to participate in activities for the better of the community.

In the last-resort situation, where a free society needs defending against an enemy, a person suffering from a debilitating addiction may choose to leave the defending to others. At that point, he has fully surrendered his responsible citizenship: he has shuffled the burden of protecting and preserving liberty, and the duty to support those who depend on him, onto the shoulders of others.

It is reasonable to argue that when an addiction degrades a person to this point, his addiction and its cause are no longer a private matter. They become political. In becoming political, they fall under the narrow powers of the minimal state.[31]

Appendix

The official poverty rate of the United States, as reported by the Census Bureau:

Table 2. Official poverty rate			
1959	18.5%	1989	10.3%
1960	18.1%	1990	10.7%
1961	18.1%	1991	11.5%
1962	17.2%	1992	11.9%
1963	15.9%	1993	12.3%

---

31. This does not mean that we shall refute the legalization argument altogether, but the burden of proof is on them to show that addictive behavior under legalization will not put freedom and prosperity in jeopardy.

1964	15.0%	1994	11.6%
1965	13.9%	1995	10.8%
1966	11.8%	1996	11.0%
1967	11.4%	1997	10.3%
1968	10.0%	1998	10.0%
1969	9.7%	1999	9.3%
1970	10.1%	2000	8.7%
1971	10.0%	2001	9.2%
1972	9.3%	2002	9.6%
1973	8.8%	2003	10.0%
1974	8.8%	2004	10.2%
1975	9.7%	2005	9.9%
1976	9.4%	2006	9.8%
1977	9.3%	2007	9.8%
1978	9.1%	2008	10.3%
1979	9.2%	2009	11.1%
1980	10.3%	2010	11.8%
1981	11.2%	2011	11.8%
1982	12.2%	2012	11.8%
1983	12.3%	2013	11.7%
1984	11.6%	2014	11.6%
1985	11.4%	2015	10.4%
1986	10.9%	2016	9.8%
1987	10.7%	2017	9.3%
1988	10.4%		

10

In Conclusion

As America approaches her 250th birthday on July 4, 2026, she is faced with an existential choice: will she become an egalitarian welfare state that pursues social justice, or will she resurrect the values of American liberty embedded in her founding?

The question before our country rises to a prominence that few peacetime challenges have posed. Yet so far, the debate of our country's future has been limited to either of two topics: homeland security or expansion of the welfare state. The former question is understandable in light of the 9/11 terror attacks and their aftermath; yet limiting America's future existence to a matter of military strength and victory is to reduce our constitutional republic below its exceptional status in human history. While strong national security is a necessary condition for the survival of any nation, it can never be a sufficient condition.

It is here that the question of the expanding welfare state emerges at the forefront of what must be a conversation on our nation's character—her very heart, soul and survival. The United States of America has never quite become the transplant of European egalitarianism that some have sought to create. The social, cultural and economic genome from America's founding remain alive in our country today. Our heritage from those who penned our nation's founding documents has been bruised, battered and subjected to formidable challenges. Yet despite the struggle for America's character that has been going on for a third of her existence, the legacy of liberty remains strong.

It is quite possible that the spirit from the Founding Fathers is on its last stretch. Currently, opinion polls show that half of all Americans have favorable views of ideas—collected under the common label "socialism"—that are in direct opposition to what our country was created to be. Influential egalitarians, some of them high-ranking in the Democrat party and therefore within an arm's reach of decisive political power, make strenuous efforts to add the final components to the welfare-state edifice whose cornerstones were laid with the War on Poverty.

If they succeed, social justice will finally replace liberty as the defining character trait of the United States. Our nation's future will be defined not by the pursuit of happiness, but by the provision of happiness. It would end America's era as an exceptional experiment in human achievement; the consequences would be felt for generations to come, and across a world where America invokes both envy and inspiration.

Only the American people can answer the question of what will define our nation's character in the next 250 years. The choice is clear; the difference between the alternatives—God and liberty or egalitarianism and social justice—is vast enough that on whichever side our country comes down, it will affect each and everyone of us. Therefore, nobody can afford to lay idle. It is our civic duty to decide what path our country should choose.

References

Alchian, A. Uncertainty, Evolution, and Economic Theory, *The Journal of Political Economy*, Vol. 58, Issue 3 (Jun., 1950), pp. 211–221.
Arrow, K.J. Some Ordinalist-Utilitarian Notes on Rawls's Theory of Justice by John Rawls, *The Journal of Philosophy*, Vol. 70, No. 9 (May 10, 1973), pp. 245–263.
Bagus, P. *The Myth of Austerity*. The Cobden Centre, November 30, 2012.
Barry, B. John Rawls and the Priority of Liberty, *Philosophy & Public Affairs*, Vol. 2, No. 3 (Spring, 1973), pp. 274–290.
Bentley, D.J. *John Rawls: A Theory of Justice*. University of Pennsylvania Law Review, Vol. 121, No. 5 (May, 1973), pp. 1070–1078.
Binswanger, H. Altruism Smothers a Republican Revolution – Again, *The Objective Standard*, Vol. 12, No. 3 (Fall, 2017), pp. 44–45.
Blaug, R. John Rawls and the Protection of Liberty, *Social Theory and Practice*, Vol. 12, No. 2 (Summer, 1986), pp. 241–258.
Bowie, N.E. Some Comments on Rawls' Theory of Justice, *Social Theory and Practice*, Vol. 3, No. 1, A Special Issue on John Rawls' "A Theory of Justice" (Spring, 1974), pp. 65–74.
Brooks, A.C. *Who Really Cares: America's Charity Divide*. New York: Basic Books 2006.
Daniels, N. On Liberty and Inequality in Rawls, Social Theory and Practice, Vol. 3, No. 2 (Fall, 1974), pp. 149–159.
Feldman, et al. *Economic Development: A Definition and Model for Investment*. United States Economic Development Administration, 2014.
Galbraith, J.K. *Economics and the Public Purpose*. New York: Signet, 1973.
Galbraith, J.K. *The Affluent Society and Other Writings*. New York: The Library of America, 2010.
Gill, E.R. Choice Is Not Enough, *The Western Political Quarterly*, Vol. 29, No. 2 (Jun., 1976), pp. 195–196.
Goff, E.L. Justice as Fairness: The Practice of Social Science in a Rawlsian Model, *Social Research*, Vol. 50, No. 1 (Spring, 1983), pp. 81–97.
Gorr, M. Rawls on Natural Inequality, *The Philosophical Quarterly (1950-)*, Vol. 33, No. 130 (Jan., 1983), pp. 1–18.
Hart, H.L.A. Rawls on Liberty and Its Priority. *The University of Chicago Law Review*. Vol. 40, No. 3 (Spring, 1973), pp. 534–555.
Higgs, R: *How FDR Made the Depression Worse*, The Free Market 13, No. 2, 1995.
Huntford, R. *The New Totalitarians*. London: Stein and Day, 1972.
Johnson, K. Government by Insurance Company: The Antipolitical Philosophy of Robert Nozick, *The Western Political Quarterly*, Vol. 29, No. 2 (Jun., 1976), pp. 177–188.

References

Keynes, J.M. *The General Theory of Employment, Interest and Money*. London: Macmillan, 1936.

Larson, S.R. *Ending the Welfare State: A Path to Limited Government That Won't Leave the Poor Behind*. Denver: Outskirts Press, 2012.

Larson, S.R. *Industrial Poverty: Yesterday Sweden, Today Europe, Tomorrow America*. Farnham: Gower, 2014.

Larson, S.R. *The Rise of Big Government: How Egalitarianism Conquered America*. Abingdon: Routledge, 2018.

Larson, S.R. Fiscal Crisis in America, Part 1: Is A U.S. "Greek" Economic Disaster Possible? *Prosperitas* (July, 2018a), Vol. XII, Issue II.

Larson, S.R. Fiscal Crisis in America, Part 2: Greece – A Harbinger for the United States? *Prosperitas* (August, 2018b), Vol. XII, Issue III.

Lessnoff, M. Barry on Rawls' Priority of Liberty, *Philosophy & Public Affairs*, Bol. 4, No. 1 (Autumn, 1974), pp. 100–114.

McCoy, T.R. Comment on John Rawls' "A Theory of Justice", *Soundings: An Interdisciplinary Journal*, Vol. 56, No. 3 (Fall, 1973), pp. 349–358.

Orient, J.M. Your Money and Your Life: The Price of "Universal Health Care," *The Freeman*, Foundation for Economic Education, December 2006.

Rawls, J. Justice as Fairness. *The Journal of Philosophy*, Vol. 54, No. 22, American Philosophical Association Eastern Division: Symposium Papers (Oct. 24, 1957), pp. 653–662.

Scanlon, T.M. Rawls' Theory of Justice, *University of Pennsylvania Law Review*, Vol. 121, No. 5 (May, 1973), pp. 1020–1069.

Schaar, J.H. Reflections on Rawls' Theory of Justice, *Social Theory and Practice*, Vol. 3, No. 1, A Special Issue on John Rawls' "A Theory of Justice" (Spring, 1974), pp. 75–100.

Schackle, G.L.S. *Epistemics and Economics*. New Brunswick: Transaction Publishers, 1992.

Steinberger, P.J. A Fallacy in Rawls's Theory of Justice, *The Review of Politics*, Vol. 51, No. 1 (Winter, 1989), pp. 55–69.

Tanner, M. *The Inclusive Economy: How to Bring Wealth to America's Poor*. Washington: Cato Institute, 2018.

Wolfe, C. *Libertarians and the Constitution*. Foundation for Economic Education, September 1956. Available at: https://fee.org/articles/libertarians-and-the-constitution/

Worland, S.T. The Economic Significance of John Rawls' "A Theory of Justice", *Nebraska Journal of Economics and Business*, Vol. 12, No. 4, Midwest Economics Association Papers (Autumn, 1973), pp. 119–126.

www.ingramcontent.com/pod-product-compliance
Lightning Source LLC
Chambersburg PA
CBHW062002180426
43198CB00036B/2144